ROUTLEDGE LIBRARY EDITIONS:
ACCOUNTING HISTORY

Volume 29

A HISTORY OF THE CHARTERED ACCOUNTANTS OF SCOTLAND

A HISTORY OF THE CHARTERED ACCOUNTANTS OF SCOTLAND

From the Earliest Times to 1954

THE INSTITUTE OF CHARTERED
ACCOUNTANTS OF SCOTLAND

Routledge
Taylor & Francis Group
LONDON AND NEW YORK

First published in 1954 by The Institute of Chartered Accountants of Scotland
First reissued in 1984 by Garland Publishing, Inc.

This edition first published in 2021
by Routledge
2 Park Square, Milton Park, Abingdon, Oxon OX14 4RN

and by Routledge
52 Vanderbilt Avenue, New York, NY 10017

Routledge is an imprint of the Taylor & Francis Group, an informa business

British Library Cataloguing in Publication Data
A catalogue record for this book is available from the British Library

ISBN: 978-0-367-33564-9 (Set)
ISBN: 978-1-00-304636-3 (Set) (ebk)
ISBN: 978-0-367-51188-3 (Volume 29) (hbk)
ISBN: 978-1-00-305275-3 (Volume 29) (ebk)

A History of the Chartered Accountants of Scotland
From the Earliest Times to 1954

The Institute of Chartered Accountants of Scotland

GARLAND PUBLISHING, INC.
NEW YORK & LONDON
1984

For a complete list of the titles in this series
see the final pages of this volume.

This facsimile has been made from a copy in the library of
the American Institute of Certified Public Accountants.

Reprinted by permission of The Institute of
Chartered Accountants of Scotland.

First published in 1954 by The Institute of
Chartered Accountants of Scotland.

Libary of Congress Cataloging in Publication Data
Main entry under title:
A History of the Chartered Accountants of Scotland from
earliest times to 1954.

(Accounting history and the development of a
profession)
Reprint. Originally published: Edinburgh :
Institute of Chartered Accountants of Scotland, 1954.
1. Institute of Chartered Accountants of Scotland—
History. I. Institute of Chartered Accountants of
Scotland. II. Series.
HF5601.I777H57 1984 657'.06'0411 83-49112
ISBN 0-8240-6328-7 (alk. paper)

The volumes in this series are printed on
acid-free, 250-year-life paper.

Printed in the United States of America

A HISTORY

OF

THE CHARTERED ACCOUNTANTS OF SCOTLAND

THE ARMS OF THE INSTITUTE OF CHARTERED ACCOUNTANTS OF SCOTLAND

A HISTORY

OF

THE CHARTERED ACCOUNTANTS OF SCOTLAND

FROM THE EARLIEST TIMES TO 1954

Written and published on the occasion of the Centenary of their Institute

QUÆRE VERUM

THE INSTITUTE OF CHARTERED ACCOUNTANTS OF SCOTLAND
EDINBURGH 1954

CONTENTS

LIST OF ILLUSTRATIONS

LIST OF ILLUSTRATIONS

FOREWORD

THE Institute of Chartered Accountants of Scotland is believed to be the oldest existing accountancy body in the world and in 1954 it celebrates its Centenary. Recognising the importance of this event in the history of the accountancy profession, the Council of the Institute has decided that it should be marked by a programme of celebrations in Edinburgh from June 16 to June 18, 1954, and that this book should be published so as to give some account of the history of the chartered accountants of Scotland from the beginnings of the profession in the latter part of the seventeenth century until the present time.

The first Royal Charter granted to an accountancy body in the United Kingdom was that granted in 1854 which incorporated The Society of Accountants in Edinburgh. This Charter still remains in force. In 1855 a Royal Charter was granted which incorporated The Institute of Accountants and Actuaries in Glasgow, and in 1867 there was granted the Royal Charter which incorporated The Society of Accountants in Aberdeen. In 1951, when the members of the three Societies decided to amalgamate, the Glasgow Institute and the Aberdeen Society surrendered their Charters and a Supplementary Charter was granted which provided that the name of The Society of Accountants in Edinburgh should be changed to The Institute of Chartered Accountants of Scotland and that the members of the former Glasgow Institute and Aberdeen Society should become members of the united body now known as The Institute of Chartered Accountants of Scotland.

In 1904 and 1905 the Edinburgh Society and the Glasgow Institute celebrated their respective jubilees and to mark those occasions there was published A HISTORY OF ACCOUNTING

AND ACCOUNTANTS, edited by the late Richard Brown, C.A., then Secretary of The Society of Accountants in Edinburgh. This valuable book not only dealt with the origin and growth of the accountancy profession in Scotland but also included a history of accounts, auditing and book-keeping throughout the world from the earliest times; it also contained appendices giving details of early practitioners of accountancy and of authors on accountancy subjects.

When considering the scope of the present volume the Centenary Committee appointed by the Council of the Institute decided at the outset that, having regard to the vast growth of the accountancy profession throughout the world during the past fifty years, it would not be practicable to follow the precedent set by Richard Brown and attempt to cover the wide field of the jubilee volume. The Committee accordingly decided that the present work should be confined to the history of the accountancy profession in Scotland.

In the scheme of the present book the first three chapters, which contain some material taken from the jubilee volume, deal with the history of Scottish accountants from the earliest times to 1905; Chapter IV tells the story of the last fifty years; Chapter V reviews the position of the practising accountant at the present day and gives some account of the work of the Institute; Chapter VI discusses the position of the accountant in commerce, industry or government service; Chapter VII deals with the training and examination of the apprentice chartered accountant; Chapter VIII gives some account of the history of the Institute's halls and libraries; and Chapter IX contains some thoughts on the history of the profession, its present position and its future.

The appendices contain lists of present and past office-bearers, certain statistical information which it seems valuable to record at the present time, and some particulars of the ceremonies and functions which are to be held to celebrate the Institute's Centenary. The illustrations have been selected to depict not only the Institute's premises and some of the office-bearers, but also a few of the men whose creative work in the past contributed greatly towards laying the foundations of the accountancy profession and of The Institute of Chartered Accountants of Scotland.

The authors of the book remain anonymous. Many hands have contributed to its compilation and to the research which has made the book possible. To the contributors and to all who have helped with valuable suggestions the Council of the Institute records its grateful thanks for their unselfish labours.

By order of the Council of the Institute,

E. H. V. McDOUGALL,
Secretary.

27 QUEEN STREET,
EDINBURGH 2.

May 1954.

CHAPTER I

THE ORIGINS OF ACCOUNTANCY AS A PROFESSION IN SCOTLAND

THE origins of the profession of an accountant lie far back in history. In the great mercantile nations of antiquity, accounts and records were kept in one form or another from very early times, and the presentation and auditing of accounts were practised by persons whom we can recognise as accountants, as we understand the term to-day. By mediæval times the art of numeration, which called for special skill before the general adoption of arabic numerals, and the art of keeping accounts were subjects covered by an extensive literature: indeed, most of the basic principles, and many of the legal principles, involved in accounting questions were established many centuries ago.

Although the history of accounting and accountants is thus a long one, the importance of the subject and of the profession have fluctuated through history with the fortunes and trading activities of nations. In the British Isles there are long periods during which accountancy as a subject and as a profession, although never actually disappearing, seems to have been of little importance in the affairs of the community. It is with the growth of international trading from the sixteenth century onwards and with the increase in the size of business enterprises that is associated with the Industrial Revolution that accountancy once more rises to prominence. This process has continued into modern times when the increasing complexity of business relationships and of monetary and taxation systems has made indispensable a proper system of accounting.

The organisation of the accountancy profession, in which Scotland gave the lead to the modern world, took place about the middle of the nineteenth century, but before that time there had been professional accountants in Scotland. The events leading up to the organisation of the professional Societies are described in Chapter II of this book, and the purpose of the present chapter is to trace back in Scotland the origins from which the profession arose until the time when it came to be regarded as a distinct and separate calling.

Every writer on the origins of accounting and accountancy in Scotland must acknowledge his indebtedness to the late Dr David Murray, whose book, CHAPTERS IN THE HISTORY OF BOOK-KEEPING, ACCOUNTANCY & COMMERCIAL ARITHMETIC, is a monument of patient research, which occupied its distinguished author over a period of many years. Much of the information in the present chapter is derived from this book.

The earliest, or primary, meaning of the word "accountant" or "accomptant" is one who is accountable—that is, liable or responsible to account; and in this sense the word is to be found in early Revenue practice and statutes, where references to "publick accountants" are made and the duties of these officials regulated. Similarly, in a general sense, anyone who keeps an account is an "accountant" in a question with the person to whom he accounts. But since a knowledge of commercial arithmetic — a subject which up to the end of the seventeenth century was much more complicated than it is to-day—was fundamental among the qualifications of a good book-keeper, the term "accountant" came to be applied to a book-keeper skilled in accounts, and from the sixteenth century this meaning is frequently employed both in Scotland and England.

It is quite easy to follow an early extension of the word "accountant" to those who for their living taught commercial arithmetic and the art or mystery of book-keeping by the double-entry method. The growth in magnitude of trading transactions, particularly in England, from the sixteenth and seventeenth centuries created a demand for book-keepers, and numerous schools were opened and text books written on the subject about this time. Certain of these older teachers developed a skill in their subject which led to their being employed as specialists to adjust books and accounts, and these men form one, but only one, of the roots from which the profession of accountancy emerges in Scotland and elsewhere during the latter part of the seventeenth century.

The researches of the Scottish History Society have brought to light an interesting example of an early Scottish accountant who is considered by Dr Murray to be one of the first of whom we have record who was employed professionally. In the minute-book of the New Mills Cloth Manufactory, Haddingtonshire,[1] covering the years 1681-1703, there are many references to Alexander Herreot, or Heriot, in connection with the accounts of the company. It appears that he was a stockholder and by profession a book-keeper, although he was not in the whole-time employment of the company. He had a yearly engagement at a salary of £10 per annum, with expenses, and he appears to have been called in from time to time to adjust entries, examine accounts, check balances and cash, and supervise stocktaking. Some of the entries referring to him are as follows: "Recommends to the Generall meeting to appoynt the Manadgers or any three or four of the proprietors to reveise the books, and to give orders to Alexander Herreot, bookeeper, to adjust seaverall accompts that are not yet fully instructed and documented"; "Orders Alexander Hereot to cary up any articles mentioned in James Ritchie's Scroll book that are not caryed forward by him before his death"; "Orders Alexander Herreot to state Mr Mureisone's accompt with the Company, to know quhat ballance is resting him"—and three weeks later it is recorded that a report was submitted.

Alexander Heriot was well established in 1697 as a teacher of book-keeping in Edinburgh, where he lived "in a little Closs on the East Side next to the foot of Bell's Wynd." He was the author of a book of mercantile tables which he dedicated to the Lord Provost and Members of Council "of the Ancient and most Famous Good Town of Edinburgh," and in the introduction he states that he had "these several years byegone"

[1] THE RECORDS OF A SCOTTISH CLOTH MANUFACTORY AT NEW MILLS, HADDINGTONSHIRE. 1681-1703. Edited by W. R. Scott. M.A.. D.Phil.. Litt.D.. Edinburgh. 1905. 8vo.

taught book-keeping and had applied himself "to find out and give easy directions for Compt and Reckoning."

The second root which may be traced in the development of accountancy as a profession in Scotland is found also in Edinburgh. Towards the end of the seventeenth and at the beginning of the eighteenth century, many complicated questions began to arise for the determination of the Courts in connection with the rights of creditors in mercantile insolvencies and the claims of various parties, some with security and some without, on the estates of landed proprietors who had become insolvent. One of the most important of the Bankruptcy Statutes was passed by the Scottish Parliament in 1696. Numerous cases came before the Courts and it was in this period that there began to evolve many of the principles and methods of ranking which were ultimately established. It became the practice of the Court to remit to an accountant, as a man of integrity, judgment and experience, "to consider the whole accompts and to state the points in controversy and to prepare minutes for the Lord Ordinary," or, in other words, to prepare a scheme of ranking and division for submission to the Court.

It is probably for this reason that from its earliest days the accountancy profession in Edinburgh has been associated with the profession of law. Frequently the designation of Writer is applied in one place to an individual who is elsewhere described as an Accountant, and there are several instances of members of the Society of Writers to the Signet practising as accountants. There is, of course, even to this day a common field of work for solicitors and accountants, but there is no doubt that in the eighteenth century in Edinburgh much of the work now done by accountants was then done in solicitors' offices.

The records of the Courts illustrate very fully the work done by accountants in these matters during the period. Many such cases, some important and some relatively small, occupied the Courts at this time, sometimes for long periods, and there are numerous references in Dr Murray's book to these litigations

JOHN L. SOMERVILLE, F.R.S.E.

President, The Institute of Chartered Accountants of Scotland
1953-4 and 1954-5

SIR IAN BOLTON, BT., O.B.E., L.L., J.P.

Vice-President, The Institute of Chartered Accountants of Scotland 1953-4 and 1954-5

and to the names of the early accountants who took part in them.

The third main source of the accountancy profession is of somewhat later date and derives rather from the growing business community of Glasgow, although to a certain extent this development is found in Edinburgh also. Towards the latter part of the eighteenth and in the early part of the nineteenth century the economy was beginning to expand rapidly and many new enterprises began. Business in those days, however, was subject to violent fluctuations, some due to external and some to internal circumstances. As an example of the former, the loss of the American Colonies caused the failure of many merchant houses in Glasgow and involved sums of money very large for those times. The upheavals caused by the French Revolution were also responsible for a large number of bankruptcies in the last decade of the eighteenth century.

In many of these failures complicated questions arose, and a considerable mercantile skill, as opposed to purely legal skill, was required for their unravelling. It was found, particularly in Glasgow, that it was often advantageous to appoint as trustee for the creditors a leading merchant of the community, known for his integrity and ability. The term merchant had then a wider significance than it now has, and the leading merchants were men of great importance in the world of business. Some of them acquired a reputation in acting as trustees or arbitrators in this way and were often asked to act, so that at this period the term "Merchant and Accountant" begins to be found. Walter Ewing Maclae of Cathkin is sometimes cited as the first to give up his mercantile business and devote his whole time to an accountancy practice. In 1793, a year of many bankruptcies throughout Scotland, three Glasgow banks were among the failures and in one of these, The Glasgow Arms Bank, he acted as trustee for the creditors. It is recorded that the winding-up was so conducted that the Bank was eventually enabled to meet all its liabilities and continue its business.

Lastly, mention should be made of the accountants who

were employed as officials by various institutions or companies and from whom originate the accountants in industry and commerce at the present day. The Darien Company, formed in 1696, had five accountants in its employment; and the various banks, and the insurance companies which were formed later, have always had accountants with well-defined functions in the preparation and presentation of accounts. While these men could not be described as professional accountants, they were skilled in accounts in their day and contributed something to the foundations on which the profession is built.

In more recent times the need for skill in accounts became greater and many businesses must have found it necessary to call in accountants of experience to assist in balancing their books and preparing statements of their position. To what extent these professional services would be analogous to an audit it is difficult to say, but certainly the accountants so consulted would require to satisfy themselves on many points that the books exhibited a true and correct state of affairs.

The joint adventure was a feature of trading in earlier days, when several merchants would join together in loading and fitting out a ship to sail to foreign parts, each contributing some of his funds or merchandise. An interesting light is thrown on these transactions by the examples given in various book-keeping text books. In 1777, James Scruton, a well-known teacher of book-keeping in Glasgow, published THE PRACTICAL COUNTING-HOUSE; OR CALCULATION AND ACCOUNTANTSHIP ILLUSTRATED IN ALL CASES THAT CAN OCCUR IN TRADE, DOMESTIC OR FOREIGN, PROPER OR COMPANY, and one example, after detailing a series of most complicated transactions on joint account, concludes that the adventurers "put the above materials into the hands of an accountant, for a true state of their affairs, in order to a settlement with each other which is now required."

The fusing of all these elements into a distinctive profession must obviously have been a gradual process; and in the eighteenth century, although skill in accountancy was a recognised and estimable quality, there must have been few men who throughout their lifetime earned a living as practising accountants. By the beginning of the nineteenth century, however, it could be said that a vocation had been established. The first Edinburgh Directory was published in 1773 and contains the names of seven accountants. In Glasgow the first Directory was published in 1783 and contains the names of six accountants. From then until now the numbers of accountants shown in these and other directories throughout Scotland have increased and it is possible to compile lists of persons so describing themselves.

Having thus traced some of the origins of the modern profession, it may be interesting to retrace our steps and give some brief details of certain of the accountants of early days who by their character, work and outlook contributed something to modern developments. Space will unfortunately permit only a short account of these men, but many further details are to be found both in Dr Murray's book and in THE HISTORY OF ACCOUNTING AND ACCOUNTANTS by the late Richard Brown published at the time of the Jubilee of the profession in 1905.

Among the first who could be called professional accountants in Scotland was George Watson, a distinguished Scotsman, who endowed George Watson's Hospital: from that charitable foundation have sprung two of the largest and best known Edinburgh Schools of the present day. George Watson was born in Edinburgh in 1645, the son of a merchant there, and after he had himself served an apprenticeship to a merchant he was sent abroad to Holland "for his further improvement in merchandising and particularly for his learning book-keeping, which then was a very rare accomplishment." His exercise books in writing, arithmetic and book-keeping are still preserved, and are models of neatness and precision.

On his return to Scotland in 1676, George Watson entered the service of Sir James Dick of Prestonfield, sometime Provost of Edinburgh, who was then a merchant of great business. There he continued as "accomptant and cashier" for about twenty years, carrying on also some trading on his own account, and probably assisting others with their accounts, because he was "much reputed for his book-keeping and distinct statement of accounts."

George Watson left the service of Sir James Dick in 1696 and thereafter acted as Accomptant to the Bank of Scotland when it was first formed. He was also appointed as cashier for receiving the town of Edinburgh's impost on ale, a position which he held for many years, and he acted as Treasurer to various charitable societies. Nevertheless he did not neglect his own private business in which he dealt largely in bills of exchange and acquired a large fortune: at the same time he enjoyed the highest repute.

"Mr Watson, never having been married . . . he soon came, by his own great diligence and frugality, to have a tolerable stock of his own," though "when his riches increased he also increased his charities to the indigent, but in such a way as little noise was made about them; which, besides what he gave at other times, he ordinarily distributed at the balancing of his books."

He conceived the idea that as he had gained his fortune among the Merchants of Edinburgh, his estate should be devoted to "the maintenance and education of the children of decayed merchants, especially of those of the Company of Merchants of Edinburgh"; and for these purposes the Hospital which bears his name was established. "And having been successful in the improvement of his fortune by the help of his education in Accompting and Book-keeping, he did particularly recommend that care should be taken that the children of the said Hospital should be educated in these arts."

George Watson died in 1723, and the notes written above are taken from a memoir that was published in 1725. His portrait is to be seen in the Hall of the Edinburgh Merchant Company.

Among the early accountants in Edinburgh, the name of Farquharson often appears. Francis Farquharson of Haughton in Aberdeenshire seems to have carried on an important business as an accountant, acting often as factor and as trustee on sequestrated estates and as an arbiter. He died in 1767 and was succeeded in his estate and in his practice by his nephew Alexander Ogilvie, who assumed the name of Farquharson and practised until his death in 1788. Reports by Alexander Farquharson on some of the estates forfeited in consequence of the Jacobite risings are preserved in the General Register House. He was trustee in many important estates and in 1782 he was arbiter for ranking the creditors of James Buchanan of Drumpellier upon the price of the estate. Mr Buchanan had been Lord Provost of Glasgow and was one of the partners of the great Virginia House of Buchanans, Hastie & Company, of Glasgow, which among many others was ruined in 1777 by the war with the American Colonies.

Alexander Farquharson in turn was succeeded by his son Francis Farquharson, who continued the business of an accountant until his death in 1808 at the early age of 36. Francis Farquharson the second was the adviser of Jane, Duchess of Gordon. The Duchess, who was the friend of Pitt and the patron of Burns, was a woman celebrated in her day for extraordinary ability and force, as well as eccentricity, of character. She wielded for a time great political and social influence and was the mother, or mother-in-law, of four Dukes. A series of her letters addressed to Francis Farquharson, written in 1804 and 1805, was edited and privately printed, with a foreword, in Glasgow in 1864 by an eminent Scottish accountant, James Wyllie Guild. The death of Francis Farquharson brought to an end a business that had been carried on by three generations of one family for the best part of a century.

Another accountant of distinction in the early days of the profession in Scotland was James Balfour, who also acted for some years as Secretary to the Honourable Company of Edinburgh Golfers. The following curious anecdotes regarding him are taken from THE TRADITIONS OF EDINBURGH by Dr Robert Chambers :—

"One of the most notable jolly fellows of the last age was James Balfour, an accountant, usually called Singing Jamie Balfour, on account of his fascinating qualities as a vocalist. There used to be a portrait of him in the Leith

Golf House, representing him in the act of commencing the favourite song of 'When I ha'e a Saxpence under my Thoom,' with the suitable attitude, and a merriness of countenance justifying the traditionary account of the man. Of Jacobite leanings, he is said to have sung 'The Wee German Lairdie'; 'Awa, Whigs, Awa'; and 'The Sow's Tail to Geordie,' with a degree of zest there was no resisting.

"Report speaks of this person as an amiable, upright, and able man; so clever in business matters that he could do as much in one hour as another man in three; always eager to quench and arrest litigation rather than to promote it; and consequently so much esteemed, professionally, that he could get business whenever he chose to undertake it, which, however, he only did when he felt himself in need of money. Nature had given him a robust constitution, which enabled him to see out three sets of boon-companions, but, after all, gave way before he reached sixty. His custom, when anxious to repair the effects of intemperance, was to wash his head and hands in cold water; this, it is said, made him quite cool and collected almost immediately. Pleasure being so predominant an object in his life, it was thought surprising that at his death he was found in possession of some little money. . . .

"A lady, who lived in the Parliament Close, told a friend of mine that she was wakened from her sleep one summer morning by a noise as of singing, when, going to the window to learn what was the matter, guess her surprise at seeing Jamie Balfour and some of his boon-companions (evidently fresh from their wonted orgies) singing 'The King shall enjoy his own again,' on their knees, around King Charles's statue. One of Balfour's favourite haunts was a humble kind of tavern called Jenny Ha's, opposite to Queensberry House, where, it is said, Gay had boosed during his short stay in Edinburgh, and to which it was customary for gentlemen to adjourn from dinner-parties in order to indulge in claret from the butt, free from the usual domestic restraints. Jamie's potations here were principally of what was called cappie ale—that is, ale in little wooden bowls—with wee thochts of brandy in it. But indeed no one could be less exclusive than he as to liquors. When he heard a bottle drawn in any house he happened to be in, and observed the cork to give an unusually smart report, he would call out, 'Lassie, gi'e me a glass o' that,' as knowing that, whatever it was, it must be good of its kind.

"Sir Walter Scott says, in one of his droll little missives to his printer Ballantyne, 'When the press does not follow me I get on slowly and ill, and put myself in mind of Jamie Balfour, who could run when he could not stand still.' He here alludes to a matter of fact, which the following anecdote will illustrate: Jamie, in going home late from a debauch, happened to tumble into the pit formed for the foundation of a house in James's Square. A gentleman passing heard his complaint, and going up to the spot was entreated by our hero to help him out. 'What would be the use of helping you out,' said the by-passer, 'when you could not stand though you were out?' 'Very true, perhaps; yet if you help me up I'll run you to the Tron Kirk for a bottle of claret.' Pleased with his humour, the gentleman placed him upon his feet, when instantly he set off for the Tron Church at a pace distancing all ordinary competition, and accordingly he won the race, though at the conclusion he had to sit down on the steps of the church, being quite unable to stand. After taking a minute or two to recover his breath—' Well, another race to Fortune's for another bottle of claret ! ' Off he went to the tavern in question, in the Stamp-office Close, and this bet he gained also. The claret, probably with continuations, was discussed in Fortune's, and the end of the story is that Balfour sent his new friend home in a chair, utterly done up, at an early hour in the morning.

"It may be mentioned that Jamie's burlesque, ' There was a Wife in Peebles,' is still well known and sung in that locality."

James Balfour died in 1795. The Honourable Company of Golfers had his portrait painted for them by a distinguished member of the Club, Sir Henry Raeburn.

In Glasgow, it is rather later before the professional accountant emerges, but mention has already been made of Walter Ewing Maclae of Cathkin, who was in practice during the second half of the eighteenth century and who was employed to wind up some of the most important bankruptcies in the Glasgow of his time. His son, James Ewing, afterwards of Strathleven, and better known than his father, though he did not practise as an accountant for any length of time, was trained in his father's office. There, it has been said, James Ewing learned his correct and methodical manner of keeping his books, so beneficial to him in after life, when he founded the great West India House of James Ewing & Company.

There are records of some Glasgow accountants who were not so uniformly successful. John Gibson commenced business in 1778 and announced the fact by an intimation in THE GLASGOW MERCURY newspaper in the following terms :—

JOHN GIBSON,

WHO has been regularly bred to business, offers his services to the Public, as an ACCOUNTANT in EXAMINING and ADJUSTING of BOOKS and ACCOUNTS ; SETTLING OF COPARTNERY or OTHER DISPUTES, MAKING OUT ACCOUNTS of the RANKINGS of CREDITORS, and the DIVISIONS of SUBJECTS, and ACCOUNTS of EVERY KIND, and in transacting every other species of business, as practised by the most approved Accountants in Edinburgh.

Gentlemen of the Law, or others, who shall be pleased to favour him with their business, may depend upon having it executed with the utmost fidelity and dispatch.

In 1784 he entered into partnership with Richard Smellie, and the following advertisement in THE GLASGOW MERCURY is interesting as giving a note of the work that accountants were then prepared to undertake and also as showing that the apprenticeship system was well understood in the profession at that time:—

JOHN GIBSON and RICHARD SMELLIE,
At their Compting-Room, third storey of Scott's Land,
Salt-market, Glasgow,

BRING forward the BOOKS and ACCOMPTS of Noblemen, Gentlemen, Merchants, Manufacturers, and Mechanics; either monthly, weekly or daily, in the most approved method; and they bring them to regular balances annually, or as often as their employers think proper.

They inspect, examine, adjust, make up, and copy, Books, Accompts and papers, of every kind.

They accept of arbitrations, and determine them speedily, according to the principles of equity, and the practice of merchants.

They assist Submitters, in making up their claims properly.

They also act as Factors on Estates and Subjects, under the management of Executors or Creditors.

They collect debts, for such as please to employ them; and they execute whatever business is committed to them, with fidelity, accuracy and dispatch.

Attendance given by John Gibson, either in the Town, or in the country on the shortest notice.

Wanted an Apprentice: None need apply unless they intend to give an Apprentice-fee.

It is known that Mr Gibson had originally started business as a merchant but had not been successful. There is now no means of knowing what success as an accountant he had, but the firm's practice cannot have been large, because they carried on a separate business as auctioneers and also, it would appear, as general dealers in a wide range of goods including India sweetmeats, Burton ale and china. John Gibson died comparatively young in 1787; it is worthy of note that he was the author of a very good History of Glasgow which was published in 1777.

Another Glasgow accountant who also wrote an excellent

E. H. V. McDOUGALL

SECRETARY, THE INSTITUTE OF CHARTERED ACCOUNTANTS OF SCOTLAND

JAMES BROWN

'RESIDENT, THE SOCIETY OF
UNTANTS IN EDINBURGH
1853-1864

JAMES McCLELLAND

FIRST PRESIDENT, THE INSTITUTE OF
ACCOUNTANTS AND ACTUARIES IN GLASGOW
1853-1864

JOHN SMI'

FIRST PRESIDENT, THE
ACCOUNTANTS IN A
1867-1869

history of his native city was Andrew Brown. He, too, it would appear, had been unsuccessful as a merchant, his firm of Wilson & Brown, tobacco importers, having failed for £40,000 in 1782 or 1783. The creditors were ultimately paid in full, but nothing was left for the partners. His intimation in THE GLASGOW MERCURY on commencing practice in 1783 was as follows :—

ANDREW BROWN

BEING advised to follow the professions of an AUCTIONEER, GENERAL BROKER, and ACCOUNTANT, humbly solicits the countenance and employment of the public, and his friends in these different branches ; and hopes, from his attention and assiduity, to merit the encouragement they may be pleased to favour him with.

Brown, like Gibson, may not have had much success as a practising accountant but he appears to have been an estimable man who was overwhelmed by the bad fortunes of these times. His History of Glasgow was published in two volumes, 1795-97, and is a readable book. Andrew Brown died at Anderston, near Glasgow, in 1816.

In the early part of the nineteenth century accountancy work in Scotland must have increased greatly. It was a time of war, when large manufacturing and trading operations were necessary to the survival of the British Isles, and after the war was over in 1815 there ensued a period of what we would now call deflation which led to many commercial failures and widespread depression of trade. The newspapers of the time contain intimations with the names of many accountants both in Edinburgh and Glasgow who were acting in these affairs ; and shortly afterwards the names are found of accountants who were practising in Aberdeen, Dundee, Perth and Kirkcaldy.

About this time too, in 1820, Sir Walter Scott wrote from Abbotsford a well-known letter on the subject of accountants. This letter was addressed to his brother, Thomas Scott, Paymaster, 70th Regiment, and concerns the future prospects of his nephew. It gives a good contemporary picture of the status of an accountant and this part of the letter may be quoted in full :—

" After my own sons, my most earnest and anxious wish will be, of course, for yours,—and with this view I have pondered well what you say on the subject of your Walter ; and whatever line of life you may design him for, it is scarce possible but that I can be of considerable use to him. Before fixing, however, on a point so very important, I would have you consult the nature of the boy himself. I do not mean by this that you should ask his opinion, because at so early an age a well bred up child naturally takes up what is suggested to him by his parents ; but I think you should consider, with as much impartiality as a parent can, his temper, disposition, and qualities of mind and body. It is not enough that you think there is an opening for him in one profession rather than another,—for it were better to sacrifice the fairest prospects of that kind than to put a boy into a line of life for which he is not calculated. If my nephew is steady, cautious, fond of a sedentary life and quiet pursuits, and at the same time a proficient in arithmetic, and with a disposition towards the prosecution of its highest branches, he cannot follow a better line than that of an accountant. It is highly respectable—and is one in which, with attention and skill, aided by such opportunities as I may be able to procure for him, he must ultimately succeed. I say ultimately—because the harvest is small and the labourers numerous in this as in other branches of our legal practice ; and whoever is to dedicate himself to them, must look for a long and laborious tract of attention ere he reaches the reward of his labours. If I live, however, I will do all I can for him, and see him put under a proper person, taking his 'prentice fee, &c., upon myself. But if, which may possibly be the case, the lad has a decided turn for active life and adventure, is high-spirited, and impatient of long and dry labour, with some of those feelings not unlikely to result from having lived all his life in a camp or a barrack, do not deceive yourself, my dear brother—you will never make him an accountant ; you will never be able to convert such a sword into a pruning-hook, merely because you think a pruning-hook the better of the two. In this supposed case, your authority and my recommendation might put him into an accountant's office ; but it would be just to waste the earlier years of his life in idleness, with all the temptations to dissipation which idleness gives way to ; and what sort of a place a writing-chamber is, you cannot but remember. So years might wear away, and at last the youth starts off from his profession, and becomes an adventurer too late in life, and with the disadvantage, perhaps, of offended friends and advanced age standing in the way of his future prospects." [1]

It should perhaps also be recorded that Scott's advice on this occasion was taken ; his nephew did not become an accountant but instead entered the Army and died a General in 1873.

[1] Lockhart's Life of Scott, Vol. VI, p. 223.

Space forbids the mention of many further names, but reference must be made to Charles Selkrig, of Edinburgh, who from 1786 until his death in 1837 enjoyed one of the largest and most lucrative practices in the country. A marble bust of this eminent accountant is in the Hall of the Institute in Edinburgh. A partner of his was Patrick Cockburn, the first auditor of the Scottish Widows' Fund. Mr Selkrig acted as trustee on many large estates, the owners of which had got into difficulties, and it has been said that his name occurs more frequently in the title deeds of properties in Scotland than that of any other accountant of his time. On one occasion he was awarded what was then considered to be the largest fee ever earned by an accountant, a sum in the neighbourhood of £20,000. This was in connection with the large West Indian house of Alexander Houston & Company, Glasgow, which became embarrassed in 1794 in consequence, it has been said, of losses on an immense speculation in slaves, in the anticipation—premature, as it turned out—of the total abolition of slavery. That failure was the biggest commercial disaster in Glasgow for a long period and the winding up of the firm's affairs took many years. Mr Selkrig was not the first trustee appointed, but a statement which was made up by him in 1809 put the whole debts of the firm at £599,751 and estimated the assets, including the private estates of the partners, at £630,331.

In Glasgow William Cuthbertson appears to have combined the business of accountant with that of a merchant as far back as 1787, when his office was situated in Bell's Wynd. His two sons Donald and Allan were trained in his office and both joined his firm; the elder, Donald Cuthbertson, who with his brother lived to see the formation of The Institute of Accountants and Actuaries in Glasgow, became a partner with his father in 1810 and was for many years a leading accountant in the city with numerous appointments both in business and in public life. He was one of the first directors, and for many years the auditor, of the Scottish Amicable Life Assurance Society. The firm of D. & A. Cuthbertson, Provan & Strong, tracing its origin to the close of the eighteenth century, is in existence to the present day.

James Kerr, who had been trained in the office of David Kay, a practising accountant and clerk to the Commissioners for the Tax on Income, set up business on his own account in 1804; he was one of the most busily employed accountants of his time and established the firm which still exists in Glasgow under the name of Kerr, MacLeod & Macfarlan.

William Scott Moncrieff of New Halls and Fossoway was a leading Edinburgh accountant from 1800 until his death in 1846, when he had as a partner his second son, David, who was one of the founders of The Society of Accountants in Edinburgh. The firm continues to the present day in Edinburgh under the name of Scott-Moncrieff, Thomson & Shiells.

James McClelland began practice in Glasgow in 1824 and lived to take a very active part in the formation of the Glasgow Institute. There has been preserved the circular in which he announced that he had commenced business on his own account, and it is interesting to compare this with the earlier examples given above. He offered to perform the following duties:—

Factor and trustee on sequestrated estates.

Trustee or Factor for trustees of creditors acting under trust deeds.

Factor for trustees acting for the heirs of persons deceased.

Factor for gentlemen residing in the country for the management of heritable or other property.

Agents for houses in England and Scotland connected with bankruptcies in Glasgow.

The winding up of dissolved partnership concerns and the adjusting of partners' accounts.

The keeping and balancing of all account-books belonging to merchants, manufacturers, shopkeepers, &c.

The examining and adjusting of all disputed accounts and account-books.

The making up of statements, reports, and memorials on account-books or disputed accounts, and claims for the purpose of laying before arbiters, courts, or counsel.

The looking after and recovering old debts and dividends from bankrupt estates.

And all other departments of the accountant business.

The practice founded by James McClelland exists in Glasgow at the present time under the name of McClelland, Ker & Company.

FREDERICK WALTER CARTER
PRESIDENT, THE SOCIETY OF ACCOUNTANTS IN EDINBURGH
1904-1907

THOMAS JACKSON
PRESIDENT, THE INSTITUTE OF ACCOUNTANTS AND ACTUARIES IN GLASGOW
1903-1906

AN OLD OFFICE GROUP

From an Edinburgh C.A. Firm

The extensive and successful formation of Life Assurance Companies in Scotland during the first half of the nineteenth century was largely organised by the accountants of those days. There was then no separate profession of actuary and it was among the accountants that there could be found such actuarial skill as there then was. Certain Widows' Funds, notably those for Ministers and for the Excise, had been founded in the eighteenth century with the help of accountants, and James Cleghorn, an eminent Edinburgh accountant in his day, was responsible for the calculations on which the Fund for Members of the Faculty of Advocates was founded early in the nineteenth century. The first four managers of the Scottish Widows' Fund began business life as professional accountants, as likewise did the first two managers of the Scottish Provident Institution. Edinburgh accountants gave to the Scottish Equitable and the Standard Insurance Company their first and second managers in each case; an early manager of the Life Association of Scotland, and two early managers of the Edinburgh Life Assurance Company were accountants; the first manager of the City of Glasgow Life Assurance Company was likewise an accountant; and accountants provided early managers for the Caledonian Insurance Company, the Scottish Amicable, the Scottish National and the Scottish Union Insurance Companies.

This remarkable record bears testimony to the skill and the high standing of accountants in Edinburgh at that time. If further evidence were needed that the profession offered a responsible and useful career, it is to be found in the following extract from a letter written in the decade before the formation of the Edinburgh Society by Robert Balfour, who afterwards became a highly esteemed member of that Society. To a friend who was trying to persuade him to abandon accountancy for the Bar, he wrote of his profession :—

"It is certainly more varied than that of the lawyer, and I believe it to be certainly not less dignified. It embraces the extensive field of insurance, which has occupied the attention of many of the profoundest thinkers that Europe has produced, and which, even yet, is in its infancy; banking, which regulates the prosperity of nations and influences the civilisation of the world; finance, whether it be the bankruptcy of a nation, or, what is often just as difficult to manage, of a private individual, and then, on the other hand, there are arbitrations where conflicting parties, placing unlimited confidence in the caution and sagacity of the accountant, voluntarily entrust him with the arrangement of their disputes. And then, just to throw a little more variety into the profession, and lessen the constant hard thinking which would otherwise be required, there are the details of general business in which most of us to some extent engage. It is here that the profession is little more than an infant one, and that no measures have been taken for reducing it to a proper shape. This can be done, and ought to be done. It is not impossible that I may to some extent be instrumental in accomplishing it, and then, I think, there will be nothing about the profession of which any one can be ashamed."

Such was the position when the first half of the nineteenth century was drawing to a close. The profession of an accountant was well established in Edinburgh, Glasgow and other principal cities in Scotland, and the accountants then practising were employed partly in court appointments, largely in bankruptcy work, generally in assisting the business community with book-keeping and accounts, and to some extent as factors on landed or other estates. The profession was also recognised as a training ground for young men, and the apprenticeship system was the method by which this training was conducted. It was also recognised that a young man trained in an accountant's office had other fields open to him as well as professional practice, and many so trained had been appointed to positions of importance in insurance companies and in the banks and elsewhere.

Of office life in those days we have little knowledge; but it is interesting to note that the professional offices in Edinburgh and in Glasgow were situated mainly in the same streets as they now are, though the actual buildings have in most cases been changed beyond recognition and though in both cities a gradual move westwards had by then begun. Communication would be leisurely, although office hours were long. The pace of events was, however, speeding up as the century advanced, and the need for some co-operation among the accountants practising in the larger centres had already become apparent, particularly to the younger members of the ession. It was realised that the formation of a Society ld improve the status of its members and that the rules he Society would impose a code of professional conduct h would be for the benefit of all. The scene was therefore for the formation of the three Scottish Societies, which be dealt with in the following chapter.

CHAPTER II

THE FORMATION OF THE THREE SCOTTISH CHARTERED SOCIETIES

THE history of the Chartered Accountants of Scotland is in the main the history of three separate Societies of accountants, each of which, very shortly after its formation, was incorporated by Royal Charter. The Society of Accountants in Edinburgh was formed at a meeting held on January 31, 1853, and its Royal Charter was granted on October 23, 1854. The Institute of Accountants and Actuaries in Glasgow came into being at a meeting held on October 3, 1853, and its Royal Charter was granted on March 15, 1855. Similarly, The Society of Accountants in Aberdeen was formed at a meeting held about the end of 1866, and the Royal Charter granted to it was dated March 18, 1867.

It was a natural consequence of the state of communications in Scotland at that time that the organisation of professional accountants, as of all other professions, should take place on a regional basis and in the larger centres of population. As will be seen, each of the three Societies continued its separate existence, though with an increasing measure of joint consultation on policy matters, for the space of nearly one hundred years until in 1951 The Institute of Chartered Accountants of Scotland was formed by an amalgamation of the three Societies.

The object of this chapter is to narrate the more important events leading up to the launching of the three original Societies and to give some account of their early organisation. It will be convenient for this purpose to take each Society in turn and deal first with the formation of the oldest—that of Edinburgh.

As mentioned in the previous chapter, it had for some time been apparent to practising accountants that some organisation of their professional activities would be advantageous. The first step towards the formation of a Society of Accountants in Edinburgh was taken on January 17, 1853. On that date, Mr Alexander Weir Robertson, after consulting with some of his professional brethren, took the initiative by addressing to 14 practising accountants the following circular :—

> 15 DUNDAS STREET,
> *17th January* 1853.
>
> Several gentlemen connected with our profession have resolved to bring about some definite arrangement for uniting the professional Accountants in Edinburgh, and should you be favourable thereto I have to request your attendance in my Chambers here on Thursday next, the 20th Inst., at 2 o'clock.

In response to this circular, eight gentlemen met on the date named. Mr Archibald Borthwick occupied the Chair and stated that the meeting was aware that various attempts had from time to time been made to incorporate the accountants of Edinburgh, but that such attempts had hitherto proved fruitless. This failure was to be attributed to several causes, but it had appeared to him and other gentlemen that means might now be followed whereby this very desirable object might be accomplished. With this view, therefore, it had been resolved to use every effort to form a Society of those gentlemen who were recognised by the profession generally as carrying on the business exclusively of accountants in Edinburgh, and for this purpose there had been prepared, and would now be read for the consideration of the meeting, a sketch of a Constitution and Rules for the formation and regulation of such an Association. It was resolved that the proposed Constitution and Rules should be put in type for further consideration at a subsequent meeting.

The second meeting was held on January 22, 1853, when a larger number attended. The proof print of the Constitution was fully considered and amended, and the meeting thereafter formed themselves into sections to wait upon those who were to be requested to join the Institute but who had not yet been seen. It was agreed that the roll of members should be completed with as little delay as possible.

The next meeting was held on January 31, 1853. Forty-seven were present, and Mr James Brown, who later was to be the first President of the Edinburgh Society, was called to the chair. Mr Archibald Borthwick, before putting the Motion to the meeting, made some preliminary observations. The idea of associating in one body the accountants of Edinburgh, he said, was not a new one—it had originated many years ago; and although the attempt to do so had not succeeded at that time, it had by no means been finally abandoned. After referring to the various important duties which the accountants practising in Edinburgh were called upon to discharge, he said that he presumed there could be no difference of opinion as to the expediency of endeavouring by such an Association as that now proposed to have those important duties entrusted to those who were qualified by their education and business acquirements to fulfil them with credit. Accordingly the plan now before the meeting had been moved in lately, and it had met with the approval of all the members of the profession to whom it had been communicated. The plan, it would be observed, was for the constitution in the first instance of a voluntary Association; but it would be an ultimate object, and probably at no distant period, to apply for a Charter of Incorporation conferring on the Institute the usual powers and privileges. The Institute would consist of Ordinary Members, being gentlemen practising at present in Edinburgh as accountants, and of Honorary Members, being gentlemen who were formerly in practice as accountants, and who now acted as managers of life assurance companies or held appointments from the Courts.

A motion that the Institute of Accountants be held as constituted in terms of the Constitution and Laws then laid on the table was carried unanimously and thereafter a Committee was appointed for the purpose of recommending to another general meeting the names of those to be elected as office-bearers of the Institute and of making such suggestions as to the constitution and laws as might occur to them.

A further meeting was accordingly held on February 4, 1853, Mr James Brown again acting as Chairman. A report by the Committee which had been appointed was made and in terms of its recommendations the following office-bearers were unanimously appointed: *President*—James Brown; *Council*—Donald Lindsay, Thomas Mansfield, Henry George Watson, Archibald Borthwick, Ralph Erskine Scott, Archibald Horne, Thomas Scott and William Moncrieff; *Secretary*—Alexander W. Robertson; *Treasurer*—Kenneth MacKenzie. The Constitution and Laws of the Institute of Accountants in Edinburgh were finally approved. Rule No. 6 was in the following terms: "New Members are admitted into the Institute at any General Meeting, Annual or Special. They must be proposed by one Member and seconded by another, and their election shall be carried by the votes of three-fourths of the Members present, ascertained by ballot." Ordinary Members were required to pay an annual subscription of two guineas, and Honorary Members an annual subscription of one guinea.

The first Annual Meeting of the new Institute was held on February 1, 1854, and at this meeting the President and Council reported that, in their opinion, the time had arrived when application should be made for incorporation by Royal Charter. This proposal was unanimously approved and the President and Council were empowered to take the preliminary steps. In May 1854 the Council approved of a draft Petition to Queen Victoria which had been prepared by Mr John Clerk Brodie, W.S., and at a General Meeting of the Institute held on May 30 this petition was adopted, and was then and afterwards signed by all the Ordinary Members, 54 in number.

The Petition set forth:—

"That the profession of Accountants, to which the Petitioners belong, is of long standing and great respectability, and has of late years grown into very considerable importance: That the business of Accountant, as practised in Edinburgh, is varied and extensive, embracing all matters of account, and requiring for its proper execution, not merely thorough knowledge of those departments of business which fall within the province of the Actuary, but an intimate acquaintance with the general principles of law, particularly of the law of Scotland; and more especially with those branches of it which have relation to the law of merchant, to insolvency and bankruptcy, and to all rights connected with property: That in the extrication of those numerous suits before the Court of Session, which involve directly and indirectly matters of accounting, an Accountant is almost invariably employed by the Court to aid in eliciting the trust: That such investigations are manifestly quite unsuited to such a tribunal as a Jury, yet cannot be prosecuted by the Court itself without professional assistance on which it may rely, and the Accountant, to whom in any case of this description a remit is made by the Court, performs in substance all the more material functions which the Petitioners understand to be performed in England by the Masters in Chancery: That Accountants are also largely employed in Judicial Remits, in cases which are peculiar to the practice of Scotland, as, for instance, in Rankings and Sales, in processes of Count and Reckoning, Multiplepoinding, and others of a similar description: That they are also most commonly selected to be Trustees on Sequestrated Estates, and under Voluntary Trusts, and in these capacities they have duties to perform, not only of the highest responsibility, and involving large pecuniary interests, but which require, in those who undertake them, great experience in business, very considerable knowledge of law, and other qualifications which can only be attained by a liberal education: That, in these circumstances, the Petitioners were induced to form themselves into a Society called the Institute of Accountants in Edinburgh, with a view to unite into one body those at present practising the profession, and to promote the objects which, as members of the same profession, they entertain in common; and that the Petitioners conceive that it would tend to secure in the members of their profession the qualifications which are essential to the proper performance of its duties, and would consequently conduce much to the benefit of the public if the Petitioners who form the present body of practising Accountants in Edinburgh were united into a body corporate and politic, having a common seal, with power to make rules and bye-laws for the qualification and admission of members, and otherwise."

In June 1854, a draft Charter, which it was found necessary to present along with the Petition, was adjusted. At this time the Council, in view of the fact that the terms of the Petition would not admit of the distinction between Honorary and Ordinary Members which had been made in the original Laws of the Institute, instructed the Secretary to communicate with all the Honorary Members to afford them an opportunity of signing the Petition as Ordinary Members if they so desired. Seven of the Honorary Members signed the Petition and thus became Ordinary Members; six did not do so and accordingly ceased to be members of the Institute.

The Royal Warrant for the incorporation of the Institute under the name of The Society of Accountants in Edinburgh was "Given at Her Majesty's Court at St James's the twenty-third day of October 1854" and signed by Lord Palmerston by Her Majesty's Command. The Charter itself—which is a translation into Latin of the Warrant—is also dated October 23, 1854, and "written to the seal, registered and sealed 11th December 1854." It was presented to the Society at a meeting of President and Council held on December 18, 1854, and to a General Meeting of the newly constituted Society held on December 29, 1854.

The procedure by which an Institute of Accountants came to be formed in Glasgow was in its early stages rather different from that adopted in Edinburgh. In September 1853 a letter signed by 27 accountants who had commenced business subsequent to January 1, 1841, was addressed to fifteen gentlemen who had been practising as professional accountants prior to that date. This letter stated that it had long been felt by gentlemen practising as Professional Accountants in Glasgow that the formation of a Society or Institute of Accountants was in every way desirable, by means of which they might be enabled to advance those objects in which they had a common professional interest. Many suggestions had been made and plans proposed for carrying this into effect, but from various causes the attempt had always been delayed.

After referring to impending changes in the Bankruptcy Law which seemed to render some form of organisation in the profession more necessary, the letter went on to say that as it would be impossible for so large a body of gentlemen as practised the profession in Glasgow to arrive at perfect unanimity on every particular point to be embraced in the formation of such a Society, it had been proposed that those gentlemen who had been practising as professional accountants in Glasgow at January 1, 1841, and who were still in business, should be requested to form themselves into a Committee or Society of Accountants and to frame such a Constitution as might appear to them necessary for organising the same, and containing Laws and Regulations for the admission of members, etc., which should be applicable to all gentlemen who had commenced business as accountants subsequent to January 1, 1841. The letter concluded by stating that in order to remove any feeling of delicacy which might be entertained by those elder members of the profession from carrying out the proposal now made, those who had signed the Requisition, all of whom had commenced subsequent to January 1, 1841, had taken this step because they believed it to be the only way in which the object in view could be satisfactorily attained.

Nine of the senior accountants so requisitioned met on October 3, 1853. Mr James McClelland acted as chairman and stated that the Requisition had been handed to him by a deputation of three gentlemen on September 30 and that this meeting had been called to discuss the advisability of the course recommended. It was ultimately resolved that the meeting should cordially accede to the wish expressed in the Requisition and that a Society of Accountants should be formed with the powers and for the purposes stated therein. A Committee of four was nominated to meet with a Committee of similar number subsequently appointed by the signatories to the letter and to take measures for organising the Society and preparing a Constitution for submission to a later meeting.

The two Committees met on October 7, when the chief points to be given attention in framing a Constitution were considered and discussed, and it was resolved to employ Mr Anderson Kirkwood, Solicitor, of Messrs Bannatynes & Kirkwood, to frame the document and submit a draft for consideration. This draft was first considered by the Committee of elder members at a meeting on October 27, and later by the Joint Committee on November 3. It was ultimately decided that the first Council should be chosen from among the senior members, that the entry money should at first be ten guineas, but that after January 1, 1857, this should be raised to 50 guineas, and that the annual subscription should be two guineas.

On November 9, 1853, the senior accountants again met as a body and the draft Constitution was approved. The first Council of the Institute which so came into being was appointed as follows: *President*—James McClelland; *Committee*—Allan Cuthbertson, David Dreghorn, Robert Aitken, Thomas G.

Buchanan and William Anderson; *Secretary*—Walter MacKenzie; *Treasurer*—Peter White; *Auditor*—Andrew McEwan. The Deed of Constitution of the Institute of Accountants in Glasgow was produced and signed on November 14, 1853. The Council instructed that intimation should be sent to the requisitionists that the Institute was now organised and that application for admission from all parties eligible might now be made. By December 16, 1853, forty-three members had been enrolled. The place of meeting for the Institute and the Council was fixed as the Stock Exchange, National Bank Buildings, Queen Street, and it was also arranged that a suitable lithographed Certificate of Admission to the Institute should be prepared. Steps were later taken to bring to the notice of various public bodies and authorities the formation of the Institute.

The question of applying for a Royal Charter was first considered at a meeting of the Council held on May 17, 1854, and in this connection there was some correspondence on the matter of procedure with the Edinburgh Society, whose application for a Charter had already gone forward. At a meeting of the Institute held on July 6, 1854, it was unanimously resolved to petition for the grant of a Royal Charter as soon as practicable and that it be remitted to the Council to take the necessary steps. After considerable deliberation it was decided that the name to be adopted should be "The Institute of Accountants and Actuaries in Glasgow," and the Petition was duly adjusted and signed in September 1854 by 49 members.

The Petition set forth:—

"That the profession of an Accountant has long existed in Scotland as a distinct profession of great respectability; that originally the number of those practising it was few, but that, for many years back, the number has been rapidly increasing, and the profession in Glasgow now embraces a numerous as well as highly respectable body of persons; that the business of an Accountant requires, for the proper prosecution of it, considerable and varied attainments; that it is not confined to the department of the Actuary, which forms indeed only a branch of it, but that, while it comprehends all matters connected with arithmetical calculation, or involving investigation into figures, it also ranges over a much wider field, in which a considerable acquaintance with the general principles of law, and a knowledge in particular of the Law of Scotland, is quite indispensable; that Accountants are frequently employed by Courts of Law, both the Sheriff Courts and the Court of Session, which is the supreme Civil Tribunal of Scotland, to aid those Courts in their investigation of matters of Accounting, which involve, to a greater or less extent, points of law of more or less difficulty; that they act under such remits very much as the Masters in Chancery are understood to act in England, and that they are also most commonly selected to be Trustees on Sequestrated Estates, and to act as Trustees under private Deeds of Trust on large landed Estates, and that in these capacities they have often to consider and determine, in the first instance, important questions of ranking and of competition between Creditors, and many other important questions of law relating to property; that it is obvious that to the due performance of a profession such as this a liberal education is essential, and that the object in view in the formation of the Institute of Accountants in Glasgow, of which the Petitioners are the Members, was to maintain the efficiency as well as the respectability of the professional body in Glasgow to which they belong; that it appears to the Petitioners that this object will be further greatly assisted by the formation of the Petitioners into a body corporate and politic, having a common Seal, with power to make regulations and bye-laws respecting the qualification and admission of Members, and other usual powers."

The Royal Warrant for the incorporation of The Institute of Accountants and Actuaries in Glasgow was given under date March 15, 1855, and this fact was reported at a meeting of the Council held on June 5, and at a meeting of the Institute held on July 31, 1855. It was decided that to celebrate this event it would be a proper thing for the members to dine together, and a Dinner duly took place in The Queen's Hotel on Friday, December 7, 1855, at six o'clock; it is recorded that the price of the dinner ticket was to be ten shillings and that any additional expense was to be borne by the Funds—a decision which, as the Accounts later show, involved the Institute in some loss.

The Society of Accountants in Aberdeen had its origin about the end of the year 1866 when a meeting of accountants in practice was convened by Mr James Meston and Mr William Milne. In due course a Petition for incorporation was presented, signed by twelve accountants.

The Petition set forth:—

"That the Petitioners are accountants in Aberdeen and are desirous of associating together and establishing a Society in Aberdeen for effecting the objects and purposes aftermentioned: That the profession of Accountants in Aberdeen, to which the Petitioners belong, has of late years grown into considerable importance: That the business of Accountants, as practised in Aberdeen, is varied and extensive, embracing all matters of Account, and requiring for its proper execution an acquaintance with the general principles of law, particularly of the Law of Scotland, and more specially with those branches of it which have relation to the law of Merchant, to Insolvency, and Bankruptcy, and to all rights connected with property: That they are also frequently selected to take the charge of landed properties and of bankrupt, insolvent and other trust estates, and in that capacity they have duties to perform, not only of the highest responsibility and involving large pecuniary interests, but which require in those who undertake them, great experience in business, very considerable knowledge of law, and other qualifications which can only be attained by a liberal education: That in these circumstances the Petitioners are induced to form themselves into a Society to be called 'The Society of Accountants in Aberdeen' with a view to unite into one body those at present practising the profession and to promote the objects which, as Members of the same profession, they entertain in common; and the Petitioners conceive that it would tend to secure in the Members of their profession the qualifications which are essential to the proper performance of its duties; and would, consequently, conduce much to the benefit of the Public, if the Petitioners were united into a Body Politic and Corporate, having a Common Seal, with power to make Rules and Bye-Laws for the qualification and admission of Members and otherwise."

The Petition was granted and the Royal Charter is dated March 18, 1867. The Charter was laid before the Society at a General Meeting held on May 10, 1867, under the chairmanship of Mr James Augustus Sinclair. At this meeting the Rules and Regulations of the Society were adopted. The first office-bearers of the Society were: *President*—John Smith; *Council*—John Crombie, George Marquis, William Milne and James Augustus Sinclair; *Secretary and Treasurer*—James Meston. The rules provided for the payment of entry money in a sum of 20 guineas by early members and a sum of 40 guineas by those subsequently admitted after serving an apprenticeship. The annual subscription for members was fixed at one guinea.

Before concluding this chapter, reference should be made to the adoption of the designation "Chartered Accountant" with the distinctive initials, "C.A." Very shortly after its incorporation, the Edinburgh Society resolved that this title, with its abbreviation, be adopted by all members. A similar course was recommended by the Glasgow Institute to all its members at the Annual General Meeting in January 1856. In Aberdeen the title was adopted from the incorporation of the Society there. Some little time elapsed before the new name became familiar to the public of Scotland or even among the members themselves; but before very long the value of the designation became apparent to all and in due course came to be one of the most jealously guarded privileges of the three Societies. When in 1880 the designation of Chartered Accountant was also adopted by The Institute of Chartered Accountants in England and Wales on its incorporation by Royal Charter, the term soon received a widespread recognition. The abbreviation "C.A." in its use for professional purposes is still an exclusive privilege in the United Kingdom for members of the Scottish Institute, and at various times in the earlier years the three Societies, sometimes acting jointly and sometimes separately, took steps to defend this exclusive right to its use as a professional designation in Scotland.

The brief account given in the foregoing pages of the formation of the three Scottish Chartered Societies shows that each arose from small beginnings but that they all met a requirement that had for long been felt in their respective cities, and there is no doubt that their incorporation gave great satisfaction to their respective members.

The matter is well summed up in the concluding paragraph of the Annual Report of the Glasgow Institute for the year 1855, presented to the members at their General Meeting held in January 1856, which reads as follows: "While adverting to these few matters connected with their past two years' experience of the working of the Institute, the Council feel that the objects of the Association are in course of being amply realised. They feel also that although not stated in our Rules as one of its objects, our Institute, while in no respect diminishing honourable rivalry in the exercise of our common profession, is yet calculated, by drawing us together for the discussion of common objects and the warding off of common dangers, and even occasionally for the enjoyment in moderation of such a social evening as the greater number of us were enabled recently to attend, to promote these feelings of amity and goodwill, without the cultivation of which the business of Life is robbed of its pleasure without any increase of its profit."

CHAPTER III

THE FIRST FIFTY YEARS

TO compress into one chapter the history of the first fifty years of the Chartered Accountants of Scotland is no easy task, and inevitably the account must be imperfect and with many omissions. The minute-books of the three Societies and of their respective Councils, the annual reports presented to members, the records of admissions and the reports of various Committees that met from time to time present a wealth of material, from which some stringent selection must be made.

It is perhaps tempting to dwell most upon the earliest days, when a practical code was being worked out by each Society and when the happenings recorded and the decisions made have an antique quality, and even a character of quaintness, when viewed at the distance of the present time. Too much emphasis on this phase would however destroy perspective and would fail to convey the progress of the profession which was going on even in the earliest period, and which has continued until the present day. For the same reason a mere description of the various differences in the respective regulations and procedures of the three Societies, interesting though it might be as illustrative of the different conditions obtaining in Edinburgh, Glasgow and Aberdeen at that time, will not in this chapter be attempted.

It has also been decided, though with more reluctance, not to give a detailed account of the Presidents and other officials of the first fifty years. A considerable amount of information about these founders of the profession and about other personalities of the early years is to be found in Richard Brown's HISTORY OF ACCOUNTING AND ACCOUNTANTS and the names and dates in office of the Presidents and other officers

AN OLD OFFICE GROUP
FROM A GLASGOW C.A. FIRM

WALTER A. REID, LL.D., F.F.A.
SECRETARY, THE SOCIETY OF ACCOUNTANTS IN ABERDEEN
1892-1911
PRESIDENT
1911-1920

SIR JOHN MANN, K.B.E., M.A.
CHAIRMAN, THE ASSOCIATION OF SCOTTISH CHARTERED ACCOUNTANT
IN LONDON
1920-1922

of each Society are recorded in Appendix IV to this Book. It must here suffice to say that each of the Societies was served by a distinguished series of Presidents and by Secretaries of outstanding ability and influence who did much to promote the interests and the public impact of the profession, not only in Scotland but in a wider sphere wherever organised bodies of accountants came into being.

The method in this chapter will rather be to describe the aims and objects which the three Societies had in common from the very start and to trace the beginnings and course of various features of the profession in Scotland which had their origin in the early period and which have shaped policy right through to the present time.

Reference has already been made to the small beginnings of the three Societies and to the relative simplicity, as it may now seem to us, of their early arrangements. In considering the early days, however, and in comparing accountancy with other professions, it must be remembered that in all these professions—divinity, law, medicine and others—as well as in accountancy, the technical equipment required to-day is vastly more than that deemed sufficient a hundred years ago; the last century has brought a progress and a growing complexity in every sphere of life. Particularly in social and business life, it has been a period of tremendous changes in ideals, in standards and in methods. The ownership of business, the distribution of wealth, the rôle of the State, have all changed; and in particular, the profit motive, if such it may be called, which was paramount a century ago and for some time afterwards, has now been considerably modified in emphasis and in application. The more recent developments in this sphere, in so far as they apply to the profession of accountancy, will be dealt with in subsequent chapters; but even the first fifty years saw great changes in business, particularly in the second half of that period. The growing profession of accountancy had to keep pace with all these changes.

From the very outset, each of the Scottish Societies adopted a comprehensive set of rules and regulations, and these, with various modifications and additions from time to time, governed their corporate existence and also, fortified by some unwritten rules which soon came to be recognised, gave guidance to the members in their relationships among themselves. The affairs of each Society were governed by a President and Council who gave active attention to the matters brought before them and who exerted great influence among their respective bodies of members. The funds were in the care of Treasurers, and from the Accounts they kept there can be measured one aspect of the growth of the Societies. The Council, then as now, was the body before which all problems were brought, and the office of Secretary was always a busy and exacting one. The minutes of the Councils form perhaps the best record of the progress of the profession in these days.

Each Society came together in general meeting from time to time to receive a report from its Council, to admit members and to discuss any problems of the day. In Edinburgh there was a stated annual meeting, but special meetings of the whole Society were not infrequently held. In Glasgow there was from the first, as well as an annual general meeting, a quarterly meeting of members, but these appear to have been rather an embarrassment at times when there were no items of particular interest to discuss. Indeed in all the Societies the numbers and names of those attending the meetings act as an index of the interest which the various questions excited among their memberships; for various periods during the first fifty years tranquillity reigned and attendances were small; then some special point, such as a question of purchasing premises or of forming a benevolent fund, or some alleged encroachment on the privileges of the Society, would arise and attendances would be swelled for a period until the matter was disposed of.

It is also important to note that from the earliest days there was a measure of joint consultation among the Societies on matters of common interest. Indeed in April 1854, after the Edinburgh and Glasgow Institutes had been formed, but before either had been incorporated by Royal Charter, a meeting of the Council took place in Edinburgh which was attended by the President and a strong deputation from the Glasgow Council. The object of the meeting was to discuss certain points in bankruptcy procedure and as to the propriety of opposing a new Bankruptcy Bill ; it is pleasing to record that after mature deliberation a satisfactory conclusion was reached. This was only the first of many such meetings, in which later the Aberdeen Council took part after the incorporation of the Society there. Indeed from comparatively early times there were some who thought that a federation or amalgamation of the three Societies would be highly beneficial, but this feeling, far-sighted though it may have been, could not be said to have been a majority view in these days.

The Societies always laid great emphasis on the professional status of their members. In Edinburgh it is true that there were the former honorary members who were, at the origin of the Society, expressly designated as those *formerly* practising as accountants but who now acted as managers of life assurance societies or held appointments from the Courts ; it will be recollected that the Charter when granted did not admit of a distinction between ordinary and honorary members and the latter grade was embodied among the ordinary membership. Apart from these somewhat special cases, it was early decided that every candidate for membership would have to sign a declaration stating that it was his exclusive object in business to follow the profession of an accountant, as defined in the Society's Charter, and that he was not then prosecuting, or had no intention of prosecuting, any other profession or employment whatsoever, either alone or in partnership with others ; this requirement was strictly enforced for a period of years.

In Glasgow from the very first a candidate for admission to the Institute had to sign a declaration that he was not engaged in the business of a manufacturer, merchant or law agent, and this requirement also was strictly enforced for a long period. An exception was made however in regard to the business of stockbroking and this arose because the men who in 1842 founded the Glasgow Stock Exchange Association were almost without exception practising accountants : of the 13 accountants who formed the Institute in 1853 ten were also members of the Stock Exchange Association. The connection between the Glasgow Institute and the Stock Exchange was a long and close one and a considerable number of the oldest firms practised also as stockbrokers; indeed it was only in comparatively recent times that this connection was finally sundered. The business of an insurance broker or property agent was not at first regarded as inimical to an accountancy practice, but this connection has gradually become of less importance.

In both Societies it was not at first considered proper to admit as a member any candidate who, although duly qualified by examination, did not intend to set up in practice on his own or in partnership as an accountant and who remained meantime on the office staff of a practising accountant; such a candidate had to wait until he was in a position to commence in practice on his own account. This rule was gradually relaxed as the volume of professional work in the offices began to grow. It was moreover the custom for a member leaving Scotland and going, say, to London, to resign his membership; this practice was before very long discontinued.

The matter of admission to membership was strictly regulated. Clearly the original members of all the Societies could not be admitted by examination, and the procedure was generally that the Council had power, for a short time after the formation of the Society, to admit as members those whom, after due enquiry, they considered to be suitably qualified. Thereafter admission to membership became a matter reserved for the full body of members in general meeting, and it has so continued until the present day, the Council merely recommending for admission those who have duly qualified in the examinations. In the Glasgow Institute, after the year 1890, it was deemed desirable for a time to admit without full examination certain older accountants who had been in practice for a number of years and were otherwise considered suitable as members of the Institute; under this sanction a number of senior practising accountants from Dundee and Greenock, as well as from Glasgow, came to be admitted, and proved themselves a valuable addition to the membership of the Institute.

The training and examination of apprentices and clerks was also conceived by all the Societies, from their origin, as an important part of their functions. This subject is more fully dealt with in a subsequent chapter, but it is here recorded because throughout the existence of the three Societies it was a matter to which the greatest importance was attached; and the apprentices in the various offices, who were trained under regular indentures, or articles as they were often called in those days, were recognised from the first as being the source from which new members of the Societies were to be recruited. As will be seen, the changing scope of the examination syllabus is an interesting indication of trends in the profession; it is here sufficient to state that the Edinburgh and Aberdeen Societies appointed a Committee of Examiners—or "examinators," as they were then called—from the outset, but in Glasgow a candidate had at first the ordeal of appearing for examination before the whole Council. Before many years had passed, however, examiners were appointed in Glasgow also. After various fluctuations in examination procedures and requirements, a uniform pattern for the examinations was set by the formation in 1892 of a General Examining Board for the Chartered Accountants of Scotland.

In another chapter will also be found an account of the premises acquired by the Societies and the formation of their respective libraries; both these objects had considerable interest for the early members in all three centres.

Having defined their professional status and having made provision for their government by Council and for the examination and admission of members, and other kindred matters, there remained for the Societies the question of the enforcement among practising members of the code adopted. In considering this subject, it must be remembered that business was then highly competitive and there was, no doubt, keen rivalry among members for such appointments as trustee in bankruptcy which then formed a very important branch of the work. It was recognised that members must be bound by a discipline, or etiquette, in all their professional dealings, and that any question of infringement of the code should in the first instance form a subject for report to the Council for deliberation and recommendation. All forms of advertisement were from the first frowned upon, and any question of undue application for business was strongly deprecated. The records over the first fifty years show that these and other matters did come before the respective Councils and that firm action was taken to deal with offenders. Having said so much, it must also be remarked that the number of such recorded cases is surprisingly few, and although the way of the transgressor was indeed hard, any action that was taken was for the benefit of the body of members as a whole and did much to establish the principles of integrity for which the Chartered Societies soon came to be recognised by all sections of the community.

A further matter which was among the objects or aims of the early members of the Societies was the provision of funds for the assistance of members who had suffered innocent misfortune or for the widows and children of those who had died in poor circumstances. For various reasons this aim took some time to accomplish, and the method employed was not uniform among the three Societies. In Edinburgh the matter was finally settled after much deliberation by the establishment under an Act of Parliament in 1887 of an Endowment and Annuity Fund, to which, on its inception, a considerable portion of the Edinburgh Society's accumulated funds was paid over: all members of the Edinburgh Society were thereafter required to contribute an annual sum until they reached the age of sixty-five. In return for his contributions a member might elect to receive either an endowment assurance, a life annuity payable to himself or a life annuity payable to his widow. In Aberdeen, the Society formed in 1902 the Aberdeen Chartered Accountants' Widows' Fund to which it became compulsory for all members subsequently admitted to contribute. The contribution was based on an annual sum with an age tax and marriage tax according to circumstances. These Funds have been very successfully managed under the care of Trustees and since the amalgamation of the three Scottish Chartered Societies in 1951 they continue as closed funds for the benefit of those who have contributed to them. The formation in Glasgow of the Glasgow Chartered Accountants' Benevolent Association belongs to a later period.

Since the Societies had been formed purely for professional objects, there is little record during the first fifty years of social events held under their auspices. Dinners for members and their friends were occasionally held both in Edinburgh and in Glasgow, and these seem to have been enjoyable and pleasant functions. The halls which were subsequently acquired were not used for social purposes, or, if so, only to a small extent. This may in part at least be attributed to the circumstances of the times: life in Scotland in the Victorian era had many virtues but tended towards austerity; and professional life conformed to the general pattern. The nineteenth century had put away the convivialities of the eighteenth century, and some of the features of professional life in Edinburgh, so colourfully described by Sir Walter Scott, had disappeared from the scene before the three Scottish Societies were formed. The days of James Balfour, as described in the earlier pages of this book, had, for better or for worse, passed away, and a professional society more regular in its ways and more sombre in dress and habit, if not in outlook, had been evolved.

But if the professional accountant of the nineteenth century was a trifle austere, he was no whit less loyal than his forefathers, and the threat of war and possible invasion in 1859, which was taken very seriously in Great Britain at that time, brought about a remarkable outburst of military zeal. In Edinburgh the accountants, with their apprentices and clerks, formed a company, later designated No. 6 (Accountants) Company, in the Queen's Rifle Volunteer Brigade, The Royal Scots —the first volunteer Corps to be raised in Scotland at that time. As was the custom in these days, the money required to clothe, arm and equip the company had to be raised privately, and this was largely done out of the funds of The Society of Accountants in Edinburgh, supplemented by subscriptions from some individual members. In Glasgow, also in 1859, the Institute, joining with their friends of the Stock Exchange, raised a company composed of members and their staffs, and the Institute gave a substantial donation from its funds for this purpose. This Company, the 17th raised in Lanarkshire, ultimately became designated as E Company, 1st Lanarkshire Regiment of Rifle Volunteers.

Both these Companies had long and honourable careers, retaining their connection with the parent Societies. They took part in the various Royal Volunteer Reviews that were held from time to time and had a high reputation for efficiency in rifle shooting and other branches of the military art. Members of the Societies bore their full share of volunteer service in other units and provided many distinguished officers in the volunteer movement. At the time of the South African War, when volunteers were permitted to go on active service, a number of members and apprentices went overseas. A tradition of service was thus begun and continued which was to make more exacting demands on the profession at the time of the First and Second World Wars, as will subsequently be related.

Something must now be said of the professional work and status of the chartered accountant in the early years of the Societies, and of the developments that took place down to the end of the nineteenth century.

Those who peruse the early records will be struck by the frequency of references to matters relating to bankruptcy, and there was no other subject which engaged to anything like the same extent the time and attention of the respective Councils and bodies of members for many years. Among the earliest actions taken by the Edinburgh and Glasgow Councils was the sending of representations to the Lord Advocate on proposed changes in the Bankruptcy Law, and the Bankruptcy Act of 1856, which governed procedure in Scotland for many years, owed something to the representations that were made. Any subsequent proposals for changes in law or procedure were most carefully watched and deliberated upon by the Councils. It follows from this that bankruptcy must have been for many years the most remunerative branch of professional work. In the expanding economy of the time, manufacture and commerce were not by any means so stable as they later became: the business units were smaller and not so well established; it was easy to start in business and, in the keen competitive spirit of the age, more easy to fail. Then it was that the accountant was called in as a trustee in bankruptcy, the appointment usually being made by the principal creditors; and the intimations contained in the newspapers of the time show that there was good employment in this necessary but, as we now see it, somewhat unproductive sphere.

The appointment of an accountant as judicial factor or *curator bonis* by the Court was often made, and this, along with the factorage of estates of deceased persons on behalf of their trustees, formed an important part of an accountant's employment. It may be assumed also that the giving of assistance to businesses in the balancing of their books and accounts and the preparation of balance sheets would be another important and increasing branch of professional activity. For this a knowledge of the business methods and customs of the day in various trades was considered essential.

For all these parts of practice a thorough training in the Law of Scotland, and particularly in the mercantile law, was deemed essential and that is why the attendance at the University law classes was one of the earliest prescribed forms of training for aspiring members. To this day, attendance at one or other of these law classes is a part of the curriculum for apprentices.

The passing of the Companies Act, 1862, does not appear to have aroused much interest among the Societies, despite the fact that work in connection with limited companies was before very long to become the most important feature of professional life. This was not so at first; a compulsory audit of a company's accounts was not laid down by the Act of 1862, although the model set of Articles contained in Table "A" to the Act made provision for this. It was not in fact until the Act of 1900 that an audit was made compulsory, but long before then it had been realised by the profession that they had important functions to perform at the inception, during the progress, and in the liquidation of limited companies. Indeed the enormous number of companies that were registered in the years following the passing of the 1862 Act brought much work to the practising accountants; there were inevitably many liquidations in which accountants were appointed, and there were also flotations and amalgamations in which their services were utilised much as they are at the present day. The appointment of professional auditors was more gradual, but before the end of the century auditing had become a steady and remunerative part of the work, not only in the case of limited companies but also in large partnership concerns. During this period the functions of registration and secretaryship in company work also became associated with the profession.

In the various schemes of company law reform which arose from time to time after 1862, the Societies did take an active interest. A leading member of the Edinburgh Society, Mr George Auldjo Jamieson, had the distinction of being appointed a member of one of the Royal Commissions which investigated this subject. Such measures as the Forged Transfers Act were also examined and commented on by the Councils.

One branch of auditing which emerged during this period was the audit of the accounts of Scottish Burghs, County Councils and other local authorities. Under various enactments passed during the latter half of the nineteenth century, a professional audit of these accounts in the interests of the ratepayers became compulsory. This work was somewhat specialised, requiring considerable knowledge of the various Acts of Parliament and statutory regulations and also of the book-keeping systems that had been evolved. It soon came to feature in the professional examinations, where it remains to this day. The Local Government Bills which were brought forward received the attention of the Councils of the Societies from time to time.

To income tax, or other forms of taxation, it would be difficult to find any reference in these early years. When Mr Gladstone in 1854 raised the highest rate of income tax to the unprecedented level of one shilling and twopence in the pound, at the time of the Crimean War, there does not appear to have been any protest from the Edinburgh or Glasgow Institutes. The years succeeding brought substantial reductions in the rate of duty and this happy state of affairs continued until the end of the century. Even then there appears to have been no employment in this sphere for professional accountants; Mr Richard Brown in his book, writing in 1904, when discussing the position and prospect, remarks somewhat plaintively, "But there are other directions where the services of the accountant might, it seems to us, with advantage be utilised. Why, for instance, should not . . . the adjustment of an Income Tax Return of profits, where a difficulty has arisen, be left to an accountant?" Not many years were to pass before this wish was gratified in full measure.

A useful guide to the trend of professional thought as the century advanced is to be found in the titles of the lectures that were delivered in Edinburgh and Glasgow under the auspices, in one way or another, of the Societies. So far back as 1869, a course of lectures was delivered in Glasgow before the whole Institute and later a Debating Society was formed. The inauguration of The Chartered Accountants Students' Society of Edinburgh in 1886 saw the start of a long series of lectures, many brilliant and all useful, which were delivered to members and apprentices and afterwards printed. It is here that we can often detect the first traces of new techniques. Thus in 1893, Mr Richard Brown, Edinburgh, lectured on Financial Trusts, or, as they would now be called, Investment Trust Companies—a movement in which Scottish chartered accountants showed considerable interest. In 1892, Mr W. J. Menzies delivered a lecture entitled "America as a Field for Investment." And in Glasgow in 1896, Mr John Mann, Junior (who as Sir John Mann, K.B.E., still happily survives as one of the oldest members of the Institute), lectured on Cost Records and gave an account of the proper method of keeping Cost Books, his main example being taken, not inappropriately, from a shipbuilding and engineering concern.

There is one other sphere in which the chartered accountant

secured increasing prominence, not only for himself but for his profession, and that was in the rôle of expert witness before the Courts. Several chartered accountants of the early years acquired a great reputation as witnesses in cases where they had to unravel and explain to the Court or to a jury the most complicated business accounts. Perhaps no single event helped so much in this connection as the tragic failure in 1878 of the City of Glasgow Bank. This failure caused the ruin of hundreds of shareholders, a criminal trial of the directors and numerous civil actions that subsequently came before the Courts; it involved a sum—enormous in those days—of upwards of six million pounds. These events led to subsequent enactments enabling banking companies to register under the Companies Acts with limited liability, but requiring their accounts to be audited by auditors appointed by the shareholders.

Among the liquidators appointed were two distinguished Edinburgh chartered accountants, Mr George Auldjo Jamieson and Mr James Haldane, and a member of the Glasgow Institute, Mr William Anderson. Mr Jamieson, and Mr James Muir, a partner of Mr Anderson's, gave the leading accountancy evidence for the prosecution in the case that followed and other eminent chartered accountants gave evidence for the defence. The liquidation itself, with its immense problems, was conducted in a way that won the admiration of all throughout the country who had any knowledge of banking and financial matters and could appreciate the complexities of the almost unprecedented situation. The crash was painful and distressing; it involved the accountancy profession in much work which was not without benefit to those clients who employed them. Although the result was not immediately apparent, these events secured much public recognition for the value of the professional services of accountants, and the increasing demand for these services, once trade and industry had begun to recover from the shock and depression caused by the failure, is evidence of this.

As the end of the century and of the first fifty years of professional organisation approached, there was a considerable expansion of the membership of the three Scottish Societies. The greatest expansion in numbers coming forward occurred after the formation of the General Examining Board in 1892, as the figures quoted in Appendix VII show. This may have been a coincidence, because during this period business was thriving throughout the country and the work for trained accountants was growing, but it is probable that the parents of young men now realised that the profession offered a discipline and a system of training and examination that were progressive and constructive. The field of employment too was widening fast. Already Scottish chartered accountants had started in practice in London—the formation of the Association of Scottish Chartered Accountants in London dates from 1898—and many had gone abroad to Canada and other parts of the British Empire, to the United States of America and elsewhere. In these countries overseas their training and standard of attainments in most cases won for them great success. From this time, too, may be dated the start of that larger movement into industry where the training of an accountant was utilised directly in the service of manufacturing and commerce—a movement that has continued with increasing emphasis until the present day, when the majority of Scottish chartered accountants are no longer in professional practice as such. It was a period nevertheless when it was relatively easy—although requiring, as always, hard application—to commence in professional practice in the larger cities and towns of Scotland with sure chances of securing a competence though not, perhaps, a fortune.

In 1896, on the initiative of the Edinburgh Society, consideration was given to the preparation of an Official Directory of the Chartered Accountants of Scotland which was to appear annually. This to some extent superseded the official printed list of their respective members which the Societies had from time to time prepared. The first number of the new Directory was for the year 1896-97 and it appeared in October 1896, when copies were supplied to members and also sent to the banks, insurance companies, clubs and other organisations. Since then the Directory has appeared each year (except for a break caused by the Second World War), and has grown not only in size but in usefulness to all concerned. A feature of the book is the geographical distribution of members that is given.

At the beginning of 1897 appeared the first issue of THE ACCOUNTANTS' MAGAZINE, a monthly periodical. The Magazine was from the first sponsored by the three Societies. It was edited and printed in Edinburgh and it soon became the recognised vehicle of official intimations regarding the accountancy profession in Scotland. As time went on the Magazine established and maintained its position as the Journal of the Chartered Accountants of Scotland.

Another instance of co-operation among the three Societies which is not without interest occurred in 1897 on the occasion of the Diamond Jubilee of Queen Victoria. It was felt by the Edinburgh Society that it would be appropriate for the chartered accountants of Scotland to join together in sending an Address of congratulation to The Queen on the completion of 60 years of her reign. The Glasgow and Aberdeen Societies gladly agreed with this proposal, and an Address was duly prepared and submitted which set forth the loyalty and devotion of the members of the three Societies and offered to Her Majesty their congratulations on the happy and auspicious occasion. Now, on completion of 100 years of its own existence, the united Institute is to have the privilege of submitting a Loyal and Dutiful Address to Queen Victoria's great-great-granddaughter, Her Majesty Queen Elizabeth II.

Thus, as the time of the Jubilee of the incorporation of the Edinburgh and Glasgow Societies approached, the members of these bodies could take stock of their position with some satisfaction. They had in their respective centres—and indeed throughout Scotland—established their profession on a secure basis. Attempts to encroach on their privileges had failed, and they had set a pattern for the formation of other Societies of accountants in other parts of Great Britain and indeed farther afield; they were now co-operating with these other organisations in many matters of common importance. They were well employed, and yet they saw new avenues of employment opening up to them, new spheres in which their services could usefully be offered. The numbers in training for the profession were large, and candidates were standing up well to the more exacting tests that were necessarily being imposed by the examiners. The funds of the Societies had become substantial, and each Society had acquired premises of fitting dignity and usefulness. The country had just emerged from the trials of the South African War, and prosperity in trade seemed assured for some time. The progress of the Victorian age seemed likely to be continued in the Edwardian period.

At the time of the application for their respective Royal Charters, the numbers in the Edinburgh Society had been 61, in the Glasgow Institute 49 and in the Aberdeen Society 12—a total of 122 practising accountants. In November 1904, at the time of the Jubilee Celebrations, this number had grown to 906, and these members of the three Societies were distributed as follows :—

Scotland	671
England and Ireland	138
British Colonies and Dependencies . .	60
United States of America . . .	20
Other countries abroad	17

The number of apprentices in training for the profession showed a corresponding growth.

It remains only in this brief account of the developments of the first fifty years to say something of how the Fiftieth Anniversary Celebrations were conducted in Edinburgh in October 1904 and in Glasgow in March 1905.

In Edinburgh a distinguished company assembled in the North British Station Hotel on the evening of October 24, 1904, to attend a Banquet given in honour of the occasion by The Society of Accountants in Edinburgh. The President of the Society, Mr Frederick Walter Carter, occupied the chair. One hundred and forty-four members of the Society were present and the list of guests, which included representatives of all the professions and from every walk in public life, is long and impressive. At the start of the proceedings letters or telegrams of congratulation were reported from Societies of accountants all over the world who were not able to send representatives to the celebrations. The toast of the evening, "The Society of Accountants in Edinburgh," was proposed by the Lord Advocate, Mr Charles Scott Dickson, K.C., M.P., who spoke of the high status that the profession had so deservedly earned; this toast was replied to by the President. Other distinguished speakers included Lord Rosebery and Mr J. S. Harmood-Banner, F.C.A., President of The Institute of Chartered Accountants in England and Wales.

In Glasgow on March 15, 1905, a Banquet was given in the Grosvenor Restaurant, Gordon Street, by The Institute of Accountants and Actuaries in Glasgow. Again, a distinguished company was present. The President of the Institute, Mr Thomas Jackson, occupied the chair and he was supported by 182 members of the Institute. The guests included representatives from other accountancy Societies, all other professions and many public bodies and individuals well known in public life. Messages of congratulation were reported from Societies of accountants all over the world who were unable to send representatives. The toast of the evening, "The Institute of Accountants and Actuaries in Glasgow," was proposed by Lord Ardwall, one of the Judges of the Court of Session, and in his speech he recalled many of the distinguished members of the Institute whom he had formerly known. This toast was replied to by the President. Among the other speakers were Sir Henry Craik, K.C.B., LL.D., and Mr George Walter Knox, B.Sc., F.C.A., a Past President of The Institute of Chartered Accountants in England and Wales. On the evening of March 17, the apprentices of the Institute were entertained at a Smoking Concert. It is reported that the attendance was large and the proceedings most successful.

One other important feature of the celebrations at this time was the publication early in 1905 of Mr Richard Brown's monumental HISTORY OF ACCOUNTING AND ACCOUNTANTS. This volume ranges over a wide field; it was edited and partly written by Mr Brown, a very well-known accountant who was

RICHARD BROWN

SECRETARY, THE SOCIETY OF ACCOUNTANTS IN EDINBURGH
1892-1916

PRESIDENT
1916-1918

D. NORMAN SLOAN, B.L.

SECRETARY, THE INSTITUTE OF ACCOUNTANTS AND ACTUARIES
IN GLASGOW
1909-1940

PRESIDENT
1940-1942

SECRETARY, GENERAL EXAMINING BOARD, CHARTERED ACCOUNTANTS
OF SCOTLAND
1916-1951

THE INSTITUTE OF ACCOUNTANTS AND ACTUARIES IN GLASGOW—DINNER, MARCH 8, 1933

Standing (Left to Right): Sir Steven Bilsland, Bt., C. J. Shiells, C.A., Sir Robert Bruce, David A. Richmond, C.A., Sheriff Principal A. O. M. Mackenzie, Principal Sir Robert Rait, Peter Rintoul, C.A.

Sitting: Lord Wark, Lord Provost Alexander B. Swan, Sir Thomas Kelly, C.A. (*President*), Lord Blanesburgh, The Hon. George Colville.

then Secretary of the Edinburgh Society. In the text and in the appendices will be found much information about accounting and accountants from the earliest times down to the date of publication. In particular the biographical details that are given of the earliest Scottish chartered accountants are the most comprehensive that can be found and are of great interest. It need hardly be said that a considerable part of the material in this chapter has been extracted, with grateful acknowledgment, from the ample pages of this excellent book.

CHAPTER IV

FIFTY YEARS OF PROGRESS, 1904-1954

WRITING in 1904 on the development of the accountancy profession during the half-century since the grant of the Edinburgh Charter, the contributor to the Jubilee Book HISTORY OF ACCOUNTING AND ACCOUNTANTS said: "Everyone is familiar with the great strides in the domain of scientific invention and discovery. These have been accompanied by a steady and rapid growth of Commerce, both in regard to its volume and the complexity of business affairs; and the course of legislation called for by the changing conditions of life, if it has sometimes lagged behind the requirements of the day, has upon the whole followed the general advance." Looking back over the succeeding half-century, one may wonder what that writer would have said had he been able to foresee the changes fifty years would bring. Scientific invention and discovery have continued at an ever-growing pace. Speed of communication and transport have accelerated beyond the imagination of our predecessors, and many of the world's greatest industries of to-day are based on inventions which fifty years ago were in their infancy or lay yet in the future. Despite this growth in scientific knowledge and its industrial application we cannot, in reviewing the last fifty years, speak of "the steady and rapid growth of commerce," unless indeed we mean the growth in complexity of business affairs and the legislation affecting them.

With all this development and change behind us, it is strange to find that in 1904 there was doubt about the future of the profession and that the question was put by the same writer "In plain language is the profession overstocked?" We may feel too that the writer's further comment, "It is quite obvious, however, that all who are crowding into the ranks cannot possibly reach eminence or lucrative employment in the profession," is indicative of that view which causes so many chartered accountants to leave the field of professional practice shortly after qualifying and to search for more immediately lucrative employment elsewhere.

Let us look at the prospect confronting the youth who in 1904 decided to become a Scottish chartered accountant, and see how, as he advances through the years, the prospect opens and changes, and his professional pathway broadens into a highway, with side roads branching off which attract many of his travelling companions by their apparently smoother surface and more delectable vistas.

The examinations of the time were, in pattern, very like those of to-day, but their scope was in fact much narrower. The syllabus then contained no mention of taxation, or of cost accounts, and such subjects as group accounts lay still in the future.

To assist him in his studies our apprentice of 1904 would have the benefit of a book published in that year by a young Glasgow accountant who was to play a leading part for many years in the training of Glasgow students and who is happily still active in the Institute's affairs. The book was entitled—in the somewhat prolix manner of the time—THE ACCOUNTANTS' DIGEST, BEING A HAND-BOOK FOR THE DIRECTION OF ACCOUNTANTS AND OTHERS IN BANKRUPTCY PROCEEDINGS, FORMATION, MANAGEMENT, RECONSTRUCTION, AND WINDING-UP OF PUBLIC COMPANIES, AUDIT OF COUNTY COUNCIL, PARISH COUNCIL AND TOWN COUNCIL ACCOUNTS, MANAGEMENT OF CURATORIAL AND JUDICIAL FACTORIES, and that title reflects, as much in its omissions as in its inclusions, the relative importance then attached to various branches of the professional accountant's work. Under the abbreviated designation of WARDHAUGH, and expanded to three separate volumes, the work is still a faithful guide to student and practitioner on the subjects within its scope.

Other text books or reference books which had already established themselves and remain familiar to our apprentice's successors included Dicksee's AUDITING, Palmer's COMPANY PRECEDENTS, Gore-Brown's HAND-BOOK ON THE FORMATION, MANAGEMENT AND WINDING-UP OF JOINT STOCK COMPANIES, Dowell's INCOME TAX ACTS and Murray & Carter's GUIDE TO INCOME TAX PRACTICE. The last named are two out of only seven books on income tax listed in the Catalogue of the library of the Glasgow Institute in 1905. Another work, by a yet more famous author, and probably his least-read book, was LAW RELATING TO THE TAXATION OF FOREIGN INCOME by John Buchan.

In 1905 our apprentice would learn of the gift of a President's badge to the Edinburgh Society by the then President, Mr F. W. Carter. The Glasgow Institute already possessed a badge and in 1909 the late Mr John Mann, on retiring from the Presidency, gave to each of the surviving Past Presidents a miniature replica of it. He also presented to the Institute the dies from which the replicas were made so that a similar memento could be given to all later Presidents on their retiral from office. To complete the story of official emblems it may be added that the Aberdeen Society did not acquire a President's badge until 1926, when one was presented by Mr James A. Jeffrey, the retiring President. These badges are now exhibited in the local premises of the Institute. In 1953 a new badge was presented to the amalgamated Institute by Mr R. G. Simpson, M.C., of Edinburgh, who was the first to hold the office of President after the amalgamation of the three Scottish Societies in 1951. This badge embodies the Arms of the Institute as devised and confirmed by the Lord Lyon King of Arms in 1953. The Institute has also its own flag bearing the Achievement of Arms: a flag which caused no little comment and speculation when flown on the Institute's buildings during the 1953 Coronation celebrations. Prior to amalgamation only the Glasgow Institute had a grant of Arms. This had been taken out in 1923 when the Lord Lyon King of Arms objected to the continued use of the Royal Arms on the Institute's seal, notepaper, etc., on which they had been used without objection since the grant of the Charter in 1855. This digression on official insignia may be concluded by remarking that the Edinburgh Society procured robes of office for the President, Council and Secretary in 1914. Neither of the other two Scottish bodies possessed robes but, as successor to the Edinburgh Society, the amalgamated Institute continues to use them and the President wore the official robes of his office when attending the Coronation Service in Westminster Abbey and the National Service in St Giles' Cathedral in June 1953, on the occasion of The Queen's State Visit to Scotland after her coronation.

To resume our story, in 1906 appeared a portent which our apprentice may—or may not—have interpreted aright: in that year there were introduced into the final examination the principles of cost accounts and statements for income tax returns and claims respectively. The subject of cost accounts was then only beginning to attract attention and, like taxation, became recognised as of first-class importance to accountants only under the pressure of the circumstances of the First World War. While all practising accountants, however, now find a large part of their work bearing directly or indirectly on problems of taxation, the subject of costing has tended to be treated as a speciality with which the average practitioner is not and should not be concerned. This attitude has had unfortunate effects both on the development of cost accounting as a separate study and on the practice of accountancy generally, but the Institute is now taking an increasing interest in the development of cost accounting as an integral part of the accountancy profession.

As the thoughts of our apprentice of 1904 began to turn to his Final Examination, he would find another fresh field of study demanding his attention. Since the introduction of the general principle of incorporation of companies with limited liability, greatly increasing advantage had been taken of the benefits of registration under the Companies Acts, and this trend was much accelerated following the passage of the Companies Act, 1908. This Act first introduced the distinction between private and public companies and until its passing most owners of "family" businesses would probably have felt that any advantages of incorporation were outweighed by the disadvantages imposed by compliance with various statutory requirements. The 1908 Act, however, removed much of the publicity attendant on registration as a limited company and made possible the formation of what became generally known as "one-man companies." The increase in the numbers of small companies, all subject to a statutory requirement as to audit, greatly extended the opportunities open to accountants and exercised a considerable influence on the development of auditing practice. So long as an auditor's appointment established merely a contractual relationship, the scope of his duties and the extent of his liabilities were matters for definition between the parties, but as auditor of a limited company the accountant found himself obliged by statute to report on certain specific matters, however ill-defined the standards to be applied might be. He found himself obliged also to form his own opinion both on the adequacy of the accounts and on the extent of the checking necessary to enable him to grant the required certificate. Successive Companies Acts have extended the range of the matters to be reported on and have defined them with greater exactitude, but the core of the auditor's report remains the expression of a professional opinion.

With the steady growth of the profession during the early years of the century, the Council of the Glasgow Institute, because of one or two cases which had been brought before the Professional Etiquette Committee, found it necessary in their report for 1908 to call attention to a Minute of Council dated January 30, 1865, bearing upon the question of canvassing for business, and to impress on members the extreme desirability of maintaining a high standard of professional etiquette in all their business relations with one another and with the public. It is a matter of some pride to note the long period between the date of the minute and the date on which members' attention was again drawn to it, and to reflect on the extreme infrequency throughout the century since the granting of the Charter of complaints against members alleging professional impropriety.

In 1910 Mr John Mann, the last survivor of the original members of the Glasgow Institute, died. His record length of membership has long been surpassed by his son, Sir John Mann, K.B.E., who became a member in 1885. John Mann, senior, had had a long and distinguished professional career, having early succeeded to an established business which he greatly expanded. He had commenced in practice in 1850 and was one of the signatories to the Requisition which in 1853 led to the formation of the Glasgow Institute. By the time our survey has reached, Mr John Mann, junior (as he then was) was already recognised as an authority on the comparatively new subject of cost accounting. The initial stimulus to the study of costing came from outside the profession, principally from engineers to whom ordinary financial accounts were not sufficiently informative. The techniques required were developed more rapidly in America than in this country, and many of the earliest text books available were American. The Master Printers' Association produced a scheme of costing for their members in 1913, but progress was slow until the necessities of war gave a great impetus to the general adoption of costing in the metal and engineering industries. A prominent part in this development was taken by a number of Scottish chartered accountants who served with the Ministry of Munitions and other Government Departments; they included Sir John Mann, his partner Mr Harold G. Judd, C.B.E., and Mr Albert Cathles, O.B.E.

In the early days of the profession, appointments as trustee in bankruptcy formed, as has been seen, a large and no doubt lucrative proportion of the work available to the practising accountant. The three Societies were therefore well able to take a due share in the consideration of the state of bankruptcy laws and of the changes proposed by the Bankruptcy (Scotland) Bill, 1913, and they submitted a report on the Bill as a result of which various amendments were made. It might have been expected that the passing of this Bill into law would have been of major importance to Scottish chartered accountants, but, perhaps mainly because of the great increase in the number of limited companies, this has not been the case. The number of sequestrations awarded annually is much less than during the first fifty years of the Charters and is greatly exceeded by the number of company liquidations.

From the issues of THE ACCOUNTANTS' MAGAZINE of the years immediately preceding the First World War there may be noted a few items not perhaps then considered of great significance, but which are now seen as the portents of things to come. In March, 1912, the Magazine noted the introduction in New Zealand of an automatic stamping machine for letters and, in April, 1913, it commented on the use of an "electric counting machine" in connection with the tabulation of the results of the Scottish Census of 1911. This was the introduction to Scottish accountants of punched card accounting, a development which has had material effects on auditing technique, on general accounting methods and, perhaps most of all, on costing and stock control. There also appeared in 1912 an advertisement seeking applications from chartered accountants for appointment to the audit staff set up under the National Insurance Act, 1911. This was the precursor of the great variety of departmental and other official appointments now open to chartered accountants.

The function of the Institute of providing facilities for training accountants who would ultimately seek their livelihood outside the profession is one which has become progressively of more importance. So, too, the number of Scottish chartered accountants practising or employed furth of Scotland has steadily grown and indeed has grown proportionately more quickly than has the total membership. It is perhaps of particular interest to notice that from 1912 onwards considerably more than half of the membership of the Aberdeen Society was located out of Scotland, a large number being overseas; this was a much higher proportion than in the two larger Societies.

One of the early Scottish chartered accountants who went overseas was the late Mr James Marwick, a member of the Glasgow Institute and a founder of the international firm now known as Peat, Marwick, Mitchell & Co. James Marwick first went to Australia to investigate the affairs of Australian banks on behalf of British bondholders. A few years later, in 1897, he commenced to practise in New York and there laid the foundations of the world-famous firm which still includes among its American partners seven Scottish chartered accountants. James Marwick died in 1939, having lived in retirement in the United States for fully twenty years.

Another Scotsman who acquired an international reputation was Sir George A. Touche, Bt., who went to London shortly after becoming a member of the Edinburgh Society in 1883. Not long after commencing his practice in London he visited America and carried out a number of investigations and reconstructions on behalf of British investors and later he founded American and Canadian practices which have attained prominent positions.

By 1912 a considerable colony of Scottish chartered accountants had grown up in London as a result of the process of migration from Scotland. The formation of The Association of Scottish Chartered Accountants in London has already been mentioned, and from 1912 onwards members of that Association served on the Councils of the Edinburgh Society and the Glasgow Institute.

The outbreak of the First World War in 1914, which has infected with a persistent malaise the whole course of the world's industry and commerce as well as its politics, had, in the narrower field of our survey, notable effects on the accountancy profession, and, within the profession, on the Societies of Scottish chartered accountants. These effects did not become immediately apparent, though there was an immediate drain on the manpower of the profession as a result of the large proportion of younger members, themselves a considerable proportion of the whole membership, who volunteered for service with the armed forces or were mobilised as members of the Naval Reserves or Territorial Forces. Throughout the war the number of new apprentices was small and the total membership of the Societies actually fell between 1914 and 1918, the first interruption of their continuous growth since the granting of the Charters. To some extent the shortage of men in the profession in those years was made up by the recruitment of female audit clerks, and some of the tutorial classes were thrown open to women to enable them to receive some theoretical training as a background to their office duties. Reference has already been made to the service which was rendered by members to the Ministry of Munitions and other Ministries and Government Departments. This reduced still further the numbers available for the ordinary work of the profession, to which was added the burden of work arising from special war-time taxation—notably the Excess Profits Duty—and the increase in the rates of existing taxes.

The strain on the manpower of the profession may be judged from the fact that the Roll of War Service of the Edinburgh Society includes the names of 171 members and 228 apprentices, that of the Glasgow Institute those of 212 members and 734 apprentices and that of Aberdeen eight members and 27 apprentices. These numbers compare with a total membership at December 31, 1914, of 1,481. Many distinctions, including the posthumous award of the Victoria Cross to Lieutenant-Colonel William Herbert Anderson, were gained by members and apprentices who served in H.M. Forces. The War Memorial tablets which were placed in the Halls of the Edinburgh Society and the Glasgow Institute contain respectively the names of 30 and 37 members who were killed on service, and one member of the Aberdeen Society also made the supreme sacrifice.

The change in the general level of taxation on personal incomes and company profits which resulted from the First World War had a marked effect on the volume of accountancy work. Many owners of small businesses who had previously accepted estimated assessments involving small sums of tax, or had prepared their own accounts and adjusted them with the Inland Revenue authorities, now found it desirable and, indeed, necessary to employ professional accountants. At the other end of the scale, the burden on large enterprises was so heavy and the complexity of the legislation so great that their calls on the services of their professional advisers also increased.

Many concerns also found it necessary to reorganise their whole accounting systems in connection with war-time contracts and to employ qualified accountants as whole-time officers, though this latter development was probably more marked in the immediate post-war period than during the war itself.

In 1915 the Glasgow Chartered Accountants' Benevolent Fund was instituted. This fund was the precursor of the Glasgow Chartered Accountants' Benevolent Association, now the Scottish Chartered Accountants' Benevolent Association. The institution of the Fund followed an investigation into the possibility of forming a Widows' and Orphans' Fund on an actuarial basis. This proved to be impossible and the voluntary Benevolent Fund was instituted which has provided timely help to many dependants of deceased members. The Association now makes grants amounting to about £1,800 per annum and its capital at December 31, 1953, amounted to £38,667. One special contribution is perhaps worthy of mention: in 1920 the sum of £236, 5s. was added to the Fund, being the amount of fees voted to lecturers at certain of the special classes for men returning from the Services which these lecturers placed at the disposal of the Fund.

At this point it may be recorded that in 1935 the Edinburgh Society also set up a Benevolent Fund to which an initial grant of £2,000 was made. This Fund granted assistance by way of loans or small grants, but the calls on it do not at any time appear to have been great. After the amalgamation, when it amounted to £3,040, it was merged with the Scottish Chartered Accountants' Benevolent Association. While dealing with the subject of benevolence, it may be noted that each of the three Societies voted substantial sums to war charities during both world wars and that during each war, as at other times, members, in spite of the pressure on their time, have given gratuitous professional service to many charities, as well as taking their full part as citizens in general charitable, social and local government work.

In 1915 a Joint Committee of Councils was set up to deal with questions of mutual concern and to further and protect the interests of the Chartered Accountants' Societies of Scotland. From the formation of this Committee, following the already well-established collaboration of the Societies in the General Examining Board, there eventually grew slowly but inevitably the movement towards complete unity which led to the amalgamation of 1951.

The first chairman of the Joint Committee was the late Mr Alexander Moore, of Glasgow, who on demitting office the following year presented a silver cup for annual competition among the three Societies in social sport. The competition has always taken place on the golf links, and at first it took the form of a team competition with only four participants from each Society. It was early agreed, however, that this did not fully meet the donor's wish to bring about a wider friendship, and the regulations were revised to permit unrestricted participation, though the element of competition among the three Societies was preserved. The competitive element has now been given a regional basis and it may safely be said that the objects which Alexander Moore had in mind have been amply fulfilled and that his gift has done much to promote friendship and co-operation among members from the different districts.

The Jubilee of the Aberdeen Society fell in 1917 when owing to the war normal celebration of the event was impossible. The Society marked the occasion by making a gift to the local transport section of the British Red Cross; with this gift, augmented by donations of members, an ambulance car was purchased. A second car named Jubilee II was provided the next year by similar gifts.

During the first fifty years from the granting of the Charters the membership, though growing, was still comparatively small and the record was strongly marked by personalities. The later history must of necessity be more impersonal, but a few personal notes may be interpolated here. The death of Mr Alexander Ledingham, of Aberdeen, which occurred in 1917, may be noted because of the link between the legal and accounting professions, now grown tenuous, which he exemplified.

Alexander Ledingham joined the Aberdeen Society in 1880, was President from 1890 to 1896, and thereafter acted as law agent to the Society. In 1917 Mr J. W. Stewart (afterwards Sir James W. Stewart, Bt.) was elected Lord Provost of the City of Glasgow. He was the first chartered accountant to occupy this high office. By an interesting coincidence the next, and, so far, only other chartered accountant to be Lord Provost of Glasgow, Mr (later Sir) Thomas Kelly, held office at the same time as Edinburgh's first chartered accountant Lord Provost, Sir Thomas B. Whitson; this was in 1930 and the event was marked by a joint dinner in honour of the two Lord Provosts at which Sir William Plender, Bt. (later Lord Plender) was also a guest of honour in recognition of the outstanding position which he occupied in the profession in England and indeed throughout the world.

There was a somewhat similar coincidence in 1942 when the Lord Dean of Guild and the Deacon Convener of the Trades of Glasgow were both members of the Glasgow Institute—Mr A. S. (now Sir Andrew) McHarg and the late Mr Thomas Hart. The first chartered accountant to be Lord Dean of Guild was Mr Charles Ker, who was elected in 1926. Other chartered accountants who have held the office are Sir David Allan Hay, K.B.E., the late Mr D. Norman Sloan and Mr Norman MacLeod, C.B.E., C.M.G., D.S.O., D.L.

In 1918 two links with the past of the Edinburgh Society were severed by the deaths of Mr A. T. Niven, the last survivor of the original members, and of Mr Richard Brown, who was for many years Secretary of the Society and from 1916 had been President. Mr Brown, who was born only two years after the granting of the Charter, became Secretary in 1892. In the following year he became the first Secretary of the General Examining Board, in the establishment of which he played a leading part. He remained Secretary of the Board until 1916. At the time of the Jubilee celebrations he was, as has been mentioned, the editor and part author of THE HISTORY OF ACCOUNTING AND ACCOUNTANTS, which was published as a commemorative book.

During the First World War attention had been directed to the desirability of providing facilities for higher education in commercial subjects, and degrees in Commerce were instituted in the Universities of Edinburgh and Aberdeen in 1918 and 1920 respectively. The institution of such a degree in Glasgow University was also considered but on this question Glasgow, contrary perhaps to expectations, took a more academic and less commercial view than Edinburgh and though there is now a Chair of Accountancy in Glasgow University there is no degree in Commerce. It is interesting to note that the Glasgow Chamber of Commerce, in reporting on the proposals in 1918, took a very conservative view and commented that "there is nothing in the commercial situation of the country which demands that our Universities should make any descent or deviation from the broad highroad of general culture which their name implies." The Chamber also expressed the opinion, with which many will agree, that what is of greatest value to a young man in entering business is a trained intelligence and a good grounding in fundamental principles rather than too narrow a specialisation.

The first holder of the Chair of Accounting and Business Method at Edinburgh was the late Professor T. P. Laird, C.A., who delivered his inaugural lecture on October 15, 1919. Professor Laird had acted as Secretary of the Edinburgh Society since the retiral of Richard Brown in 1916 and had also been a member of the General Examining Board from 1912. His inaugural lecture dealt with "The Development of Accountancy in Relation to Commerce" and traced the changes which had occurred since the professional accountant's work was mainly in connection with bankruptcy matters or remits from the Courts to the stage at which auditing became the main employment. Reflecting the current interest in costing, Professor Laird remarked the desire of traders not only to know the results of their trading but how these results had arisen and to have information on the cost and profit of different products as a guide to future estimates.

It has been noted that the assistance of women had been

obtained during the war to enable the profession to overtake the increasing volume of work and shortage of male staff and that some classes had been opened to women, but the question of admitting women members was still under discussion when the passage of the Sex Disqualification (Removal) Act, 1919, took the decision out of the hands of the Societies. Removal of this barrier did not however produce any great rush of new entrants. The first woman to be admitted as a Scottish chartered accountant was Miss Isabel Clyne Guthrie, now Mrs Lochhead, who was admitted to the Glasgow Institute in 1923 and later gave the Guthrie Prize which is awarded to the best woman candidate of each year at the Institute's Final Examination. The first woman to be admitted to the Edinburgh Society was Miss Helen Mitchell Somerville, who became a member in 1925. She is the sister and former partner of the present President of the Institute. The women of Aberdeen lagged somewhat behind in this matter, as it was not until 1936 that Miss Amelia Heggie Melville, now Mrs Kitley, became the first woman member of the Aberdeen Society.

The years immediately following the First World War were years of rapid expansion. Those whose professional training had been delayed by war service entered into indentures and inflated the number of new apprentices, which had fallen very low during the war. Special classes were held for men returning from service, examination concessions accelerated their qualification, and the number of members admitted each year was fully twice the pre-war figure. Industry and commerce, too, enjoyed a fleeting boom during which, with their wartime experience of the benefits of efficient accounting behind them, managements eagerly sought the services of qualified accountants.

The record of geographical distribution of membership about this time shows that the increase in the number of Scottish chartered accountants overseas, which had been rapid between 1904 and 1914, had, as was to be expected, been halted by the war and was not resumed till some years later. The influx into London, on the other hand, which had proceeded steadily up to 1914, was accelerated after the war. These trends gave rise to the problem of the apprentice outwith Scotland. The Councils had to consider whether it was desirable that men should be admitted as members of the Scottish Societies whose training and experience were entirely foreign (the 'Auld Enemy' with its different legal system being for this purpose regarded as foreign). In the end a compromise solution was adopted, which has on the whole worked well. Members overseas were prohibited from taking apprentices but members practising in England or Wales were allowed to have apprentices. The number which such members could take was later restricted and, as has already been described, apprentices in London were required to take certain prescribed classes in place of the compulsory University classes. From time to time proposals have been made for the general restriction of the number of apprentices which each master or firm might take, but these have always been negatived and the possibility of a shortage of apprentices rather than an excess has been of more frequent and pressing concern.

The dispersal of members outwith Scotland was accompanied by a similar dispersal at home, and the growing importance of the accountant's services to the industrial and commercial community which this denotes is illustrated by the following figures. In 1904 the Directory listed 25 places in Scotland, including the four large cities, where there were members of the three Scottish Societies; by 1929 the number of places listed had grown to over 100; and in 1953 the number was over 200, and in 95 of these places there were members in practice.

Industrial conditions through the 1920's and early 1930's also provided considerable scope for activity among chartered accountants in practice. During the boom period there were many new flotations and amalgamations; these gave rise to new accounting problems, among which those arising from the development of holding companies were perhaps most important. Accountants also found scope for the exercise of their skill in connection with the numerous reconstruction schemes which

R. G. SIMPSON, M.C.

President, The Institute of Chartered Accountants of Scotland

1951-1952

SIR DAVID ALLAN HAY, K.B.E.
PRESIDENT, THE INSTITUTE OF CHARTERED ACCOUNTANTS OF SCOTLAND
1952-1953

followed the collapse of the boom and in the complex taxation problems that arose on the termination of the Excess Profits Duty. Businesses engaged in many branches of engineering found themselves at the close of the war equipped with specialised plant which had been installed at high prices but for which profitable employment did not exist. Other concerns which had been capitalised to take advantage of the immediate post-war rise in asset values found themselves with top-heavy capital structures. Others again were borne down by the weight of forward purchasing commitments incurred at high prices when supplies were short, or were burdened by stocks which had almost overnight fallen in value to a fraction of their cost. Towards the solution of these and other problems Scottish chartered accountants made their full contribution, and, though hardship was suffered by many businesses and unemployment was widespread throughout the country, there were no major financial catastrophes such as had marked earlier slumps.

In 1925, Glasgow, although still not instituting a degree in Commerce, came partially into line with the other two cities in the provision of University training in Accountancy. Through the generosity of Mr D. Johnstone Smith, an ex-President of the Institute, who gave a sum of £20,000 to the University of Glasgow for the purpose, there was established at the University a Chair of Accountancy. The first Professor to be appointed was Mr John Loudon, C.A., who delivered his inaugural lecture at the commencement of the 1926-27 session. Attendance at this class was henceforth compulsory in place of attendance at the former special class at the Glasgow and West of Scotland Commercial College. Mr Johnstone Smith received the honorary degree of LL.D. of Glasgow University. He was also invited by the Glasgow Institute to sit for his portrait so that it might be hung in the Institute's hall. This portrait, with those of a number of other eminent accountants of the past, is a permanent reminder to their successors of the debt which is due to those who by their ability, integrity and generosity have helped to establish the high reputation of Scottish chartered accountants throughout the world.

Professor Laird, the first holder of the Chair of Accounting and Business Method in the University of Edinburgh, died in 1927 and was succeeded by the late Professor William Annan, C.A., who took as the subject of his inaugural address "The Scope for Accountancy in Modern Business." His address emphasised the increasing scope for the accountant's services which was provided by the extension of limited liability, the increase in taxation, and the growth in amalgamations and in the work of trade associations.

These factors which affected the activities of the individual accountant have all been the subject of comment in the foregoing pages, but it may be convenient at this stage, approximately the mid-way point of the half-century, to remark certain corporate activities of the three Scottish Societies. These activities have in the main been purely professional as distinct from social. From time to time dinners were held to mark some special occasion or to do honour to a distinguished member, but none of the Societies held regular annual dinners. Between 1929 and 1939, however, the Glasgow Institute promoted a number of very successful dinners at which attendance ranged from 220 to 280 and at which many distinguished guests were present. At the 1938 dinner representatives of all the kindred Societies in Great Britain attended.

The Councils, latterly through the medium of the Joint Committee of Councils, submitted evidence or memoranda to numerous Royal Commissions, Departmental Committees and similar bodies dealing with proposed or pending legislation. The Joint Committee of Councils also took action to protect the profession's interests whenever these seemed likely to be adversely affected by private or public legislation or by the action of Government Departments. One result of such action was that the Scottish Societies were included among the bodies from which local government auditors in England might be appointed, and amendments were secured to other Bills which in their original form were thought to be detrimental to the interests of Scottish chartered accountants. Representations were also made to Dominion and Foreign Governments on behalf of members abroad whose interests might be affected by local regulations or legislation. One matter which recurred at intervals and which is not yet finally disposed of was the question of registration of public accountants in the United Kingdom. From the latter part of the nineteenth century a number of draft Bills dealing with this had been produced, but for one reason or another it was never found practicable to secure agreement to legislation on the subject.

The Societies have always maintained cordial relations with kindred organisations at home and abroad and references in the annual reports to the attendance of representatives at anniversary celebrations of foreign institutes become increasingly frequent. Representatives also attended the early International Congresses of Accountants. At the Third International Congress in New York in 1929, Professor Annan submitted a paper on "Cost Accounts from the Professional Accountants' Point of View" and Mr Anthony C. McMillan, a member of the Glasgow Institute, read a paper on "Municipal Budgeting in Scotland." The first International Congress to be held in the United Kingdom —the Fourth of the series—took place in 1933, when the Scottish Societies were among the sponsoring bodies and Professor Annan was again one of those presenting papers, his subject this time being "Accounting as an Aid to Commerce." After the business sessions in London, a large party of the foreign delegates and visitors came to Scotland and were entertained by the three Chartered Societies and the Corporation of Accountants Ltd.

A milestone in the growth of the profession was passed in 1931 when the membership of the Glasgow Institute reached 2,000. The membership of the Edinburgh Society had passed 1,000 in the previous year. The number of members continued to increase rapidly and by 1935 the Glasgow members numbered more than 2,500 and the Edinburgh members over 1,200.

It has been remarked in an earlier Chapter that in the 1890's a number of members were admitted to the Glasgow Institute without examination. It is interesting to note that a few members of the Edinburgh Society who exercised their profession in the West also became members of the Glasgow Institute. The last survivor of this small group, Mr William Hardie, died in 1937, having been predeceased in 1934 by the most distinguished member of it—Sir John M. MacLeod, Bt. Sir John MacLeod, a member of a family which has produced some well-known Scottish divines, had rendered valuable service to the Glasgow Institute, of which he was President from 1926 to 1928, and to the Glasgow Chartered Accountants Students' Society, of which he had been an honorary President. He had also played an important part in Church affairs and as a Member of Parliament successively for the Central and Kelvingrove divisions of Glasgow from 1915 to 1922.

It has been noted above that the depression of the early 1930's was not marked by the failure of many large financial organisations, but a number of cases which aroused great public interest and gave rise to much discussion in accountancy circles came before the Courts at about this time. These had their origin in the financial collapse of groups of companies and involved charges of fraud or other criminal conduct against directors and auditors. The most important to accountants was the Royal Mail Steam Packet Company Case which led to the trial of Lord Kylsant, the chairman of the company, and of the auditor. The Kylsant case arose in part from the issue of an allegedly fraudulent prospectus: the main question at issue was as to the degree of disclosure required when transfers were made from hidden reserves and used to increase the published profits. Until the passing of the Companies Act, 1948, the decision in this case governed the treatment of such entries in company accounts, but that Act provided definite statutory rules on the subject.

The re-organisation of the Royal Mail Steam Packet Company Group which followed the trial was one of the many important matters on which the late Sir William McLintock, Bt., was engaged at this period. Sir William's firm was, in 1912, among the first of the Glasgow firms to open a London office and under his control a practice was built up which has achieved very wide extent and influence. In spite of the calls which the conduct of this practice made on him, and in spite of the work for Government Commissions on which he was almost continually engaged, Sir William McLintock was always active in the interests of Scottish chartered accountants and also found time to deliver several important lectures to the Students' Societies. The Glasgow Institute, of which he was always proud to declare himself a member, could in turn be proud of his standing as one of the most eminent accountants and financial experts of the time.

Of much domestic interest to the profession in Scotland was the trial in 1932 of the promoters of Scottish Amalgamated Silks Ltd. on charges of issuing a fraudulent prospectus and making fraudulent allotments of shares. Several of the leading members of the profession in Scotland were engaged in the investigations which preceded the trial; the principal Crown witnesses on accounting matters were Mr (now Sir) David Allan Hay and the late Mr James A. French.

The Companies Act, 1929, had recognised the growing importance of "holding" companies and groups of companies in the financial organisation of industry and had made provision for a certain minimum of disclosure of information in the accounts of holding companies. While some of the worst abuses which had existed under the previous legislation were thus checked, the required standard of group accounting fell short of what was considered desirable by the accounting profession and had in fact been adopted by many leading companies. In 1932, therefore, we find a Special Committee set up by the Joint Committee of Councils to consider the operation of the 1929 Act with particular reference to this aspect. Further legislative amendment, however, was delayed until 1947, but in the interval practice moved well ahead of the legal requirements. Indeed, in their accounting provisions, recent Companies Acts have merely reflected, and sometimes imperfectly reflected, the progress already made in practice.

Since the introduction of the "electric counting machine" for census purposes in 1911, there had been a steady growth in the number and variety of mechanical aids to accounting.

Industrial depression, with its accompaniment of "rationalisation" and the search for economies, had given an impetus to the adoption of mechanism in the office, and the new forms of records demanded that accountants reconsider their audit procedures. The first paper on "Mechanised Accounting" to appear in Students' Societies' Transactions was presented to the Glasgow Students' Society on January 30, 1935. In the same year the Glasgow Institute arranged for its members a course of lectures on mechanised accounting, and a prize was also offered for an essay on the subject. The development of accounting and calculating machines has continued at an increasing speed. The use of electronic devices during the Second World War for artillery and other purposes has led to the adaptation of the principle of the "mechanical brain" to commercial calculations. While such devices are not yet in common use and are likely, at all events in the near future, to be restricted to the service of organisations of great size, their development may have a considerable influence on the future of accounting and auditing techniques.

The number of Scottish chartered accountants practising in London had continued to grow, and in 1933 examinations were held there for the first time. About the same time The Association of Scottish Chartered Accountants in London considered the acquisition of premises and the formation of a library, but a few years later an arrangement was reached with The Institute of Chartered Accountants in England and Wales whereby members of the Association and their apprentices were permitted to use the library and premises of the English Institute. The number of apprentices indentured to Scottish chartered accountants practising in England had increased from 19 in 1924 to 120 in 1934.

In each of the five years after 1932 there was a continuous fall in the number of indentures of apprentices registered and in 1937 this reached such a stage as to cause alarm. A Committee was appointed by the Glasgow Institute to consider the position. This Committee formed the opinion that the falling-off was due mainly to the industrial depression and to a prevalent view that the profession was overcrowded and did not have the attractions offered by other careers. There was some slight increase in the numbers in the next two years, but the Second World War again reduced the number of new entrants. While post-war figures have been comparable to those of the early 1920's the number of new members remaining with practising firms, as distinct from those otherwise employed, remains inadequate and a cause of serious concern.

Two schemes which might have had some effect on recruitment to the profession were under consideration by the Council of the Glasgow Institute when war broke out in 1939. The first of these was a proposal to institute a scheme of pensions for the office staffs of members; the second was a suggestion that part of the Institute's funds, which in 1937 exceeded £100,000, could usefully be employed in grants to students in adversity and in establishing bursaries to encourage suitable entrants to the profession. These schemes have not been revived, but the provisions now made by the State, particularly for the encouragement of technical and professional training, have somewhat reduced the financial barrier to entry to the profession.

With the darkening of the international scene the link between the profession in Scotland and the armed forces was renewed. As mentioned in Chapter III, this link was forged in 1859, when the Edinburgh Society and the Glasgow Institute had assisted in raising Volunteer Companies, largely from among their own members. As the stage was set for the Second World War the Glasgow Institute became connected with the 57th (Glasgow) Searchlight and 74th (City of Glasgow) Anti-Aircraft Regiments of the Royal Artillery which were largely recruited from accountants and their staffs in Glasgow. The Institute presented silver trophies to each of these Regiments. In Edinburgh and Aberdeen, as elsewhere in Scotland, many younger members joined the Territorial Army about this time.

In spite of the political tension it was possible to hold the Fifth International Congress on Accounting in Berlin in September 1938. The Edinburgh Society and the Glasgow Institute were represented and a paper on "Company Law in the United Kingdom" was submitted by Professor Loudon.

The outbreak of the Second World War in 1939 had an immediate and serious effect on the profession. The many members and apprentices who had enlisted in the Royal Naval Volunteer Reserve or in units of the Territorial Army or in the Royal Air Force Volunteer Reserve were immediately called away for active service and most of them did not resume professional life for more than six years. The importance of the contribution which the profession could make to the war effort was recognised by the inclusion of accountants in the list of reserved occupations and this helped to ease the strain. The age of reservation which was originally fixed at 30 was later reduced to 25, but was again raised to 30 in 1941. A Committee was then set up to assist the Ministry of Labour in dealing with questions of the deferment of the calling up of practising accountants and their staffs. This Committee continued to give valuable service throughout the war.

As in the First World War, the imposition of special wartime taxation increased greatly the work falling on the profession. Returns that were required under various regulations for the restriction of output of civilian goods and for the regulation of prices added a further burden. There is little doubt that these extra demands resulted in some relaxation of the standards of auditing work, but in so far as this merely eliminated repetitive checks and led to a greater reliance on proper sampling and to emphasis on the importance of adequate internal control, the changes may well have been beneficial. A great deal of the war production was carried out under Government contracts embodying provisions for a cost audit, and the Ministries concerned built up large staffs to undertake this work. Not all members of these staffs were professionally qualified, but Scottish chartered accountants played their full part in devising and operating the various schemes of price control and verification which were found necessary.

During the war the normal activities of the Societies were severely curtailed. The problems occupying the attention of the Councils and the Joint Committee were mainly those of manpower and the modifications necessitated by the war in the normal schemes of training and examination. Regulations for ex-service candidates were agreed upon and announced at an early stage, and plans were made for special courses of lectures for members and apprentices on their return from war service.

A feature of governmental activity in these years was the amount of attention which, in spite of almost overwhelming immediate pre-occupations, was given to problems of post-war reconstruction. One of the matters to which attention was directed was that of post-war fiscal policy and in 1943 the three Councils set up Taxation Committees the first duty of which was to prepare a joint report on the incidence of income tax on industrial profits in relation to post-war fiscal policy. Evidence was also submitted to a Royal Commission on Company Law amendment. The discussions which had proceeded intermittently and inconclusively over many years on the co-ordination and registration of the profession were also continued.

The number of examination candidates was greatly reduced throughout the war. Certain diets of the Second Division of the Final Examination were not held and for some years no examinations were held in London. Arrangements were made through the British Red Cross for the transmission of tutorial material to prisoners of war, and it was also found possible to arrange for the holding of examinations in some Prisoner of War Camps. A few candidates were successful in passing under these extraordinarily difficult conditions and no doubt even found relief from their immediate distress in pursuing their professional studies. Another of those who studied to some purpose in such circumstances was Mr D. J. Bogie, a member of the Edinburgh Society; he prepared a thesis entitled "An Investigation into the Preparation of Consolidated Statements for Holding Companies," much of the work on which was done while he was a prisoner of war in Germany, and this led to his receiving a Doctorate of Philosophy from

Edinburgh University in 1948—one of the first higher University degrees for a thesis on an accounting subject.

During the war the membership of the Glasgow Institute for the first time exceeded 3,000, but there was later a slight decline in numbers and the membership at December 31, 1945, was 2,982. The membership of the Edinburgh Society declined from 1,334 at December 31, 1939, to 1,262 six years later. The Aberdeen Society fluctuated slightly in membership throughout the war and at December 31, 1945, at 222, had two fewer members than at the commencement of hostilities.

Of the Aberdeen members who died about this time, note may be taken of one of the oldest members of the Society. Dr W. A. Reid was admitted a member in 1884 and at an early age became senior partner in the firm of James Meston & Co., of Aberdeen and London. As Secretary of his own Society from 1892 to 1911 and President from 1911 to 1920 and as a member of the General Examining Board and of the Joint Committee of Councils Dr Reid rendered notable services to the profession, and he also gave valuable service to educational and charitable institutions in Aberdeen. Dr Reid was succeeded as Secretary by his partner Mr John Reid, who filled the position till 1937 when he became President, an office which he held until his death in 1946.

In 1945 the Joint Committee of Councils set up a Subcommittee to consider the advisability of merging the three Scottish Societies. The initial suggestion came from the Glasgow Council, then presided over by Sir David Allan Hay, to whose vision, energy and organising ability the ultimate success of the amalgamation owes so much. In the early stages of the negotiations numerous difficulties were encountered and progress was slow, so slow indeed that a speaker at the Jubilee Dinner of the Glasgow Chartered Accountants Students' Society in 1949 referred to it as being "at glacial speed." All obstacles were eventually overcome and draft Rules were presented for the approval of the three Societies. Edinburgh and Aberdeen gave unanimous approval to the proposals, but Glasgow, although the initiators of the scheme, had doubts and a postal poll of members was required before the necessary majority was obtained. The Edinburgh Society was then the oldest incorporated body of accountants in the world and it was felt desirable, to secure continuity, that its Charter should be preserved, although the Glasgow Institute, only slightly junior in age, had a much greater membership. The amalgamation arrangements, therefore, took the form of admitting to membership of the Edinburgh Society, renamed and constituted by a Supplementary Charter as The Institute of Chartered Accountants of Scotland, the members of the other two Societies, whose Charters were then surrendered.

This amalgamation is undoubtedly the most significant event of the half-century for Scottish chartered accountants. Because of the growing part which the profession had come to play in the national economy, the old local organisations had become outmoded. Problems on which a corporate expression of opinion was either sought by Government or demanded by circumstances became ever more frequent, and while the Societies had for many years collaborated through the Joint Committee of Councils, this machinery was cumbersome and slow-moving and the lack of formal unity detracted from the weight of any views expressed. In England and abroad Scottish chartered accountants enjoyed a high reputation, but this was as Scottish chartered accountants and not as members of the individual Societies. Now the profession in Scotland can speak with one voice, and the individual member is backed by the prestige and reputation of a unified Institute.

The First World War had resulted in a permanent change in the level of taxation and had stimulated interest in costing. The Second World War so increased the already heavy tax burden that the taxation effect of any suggested course of action became one of the major considerations to be taken into account in any business enterprise. Apart from taxes on income and profits, the imposition of new taxes or increases in existing taxes have added to the problems on which accountants are called to advise. This taxation work has brought about close and cordial relations between individual members of the profession and H.M. Inspectors of Taxes and between the professional accountancy bodies and the Board of Inland Revenue. It is perhaps no exaggeration to say that, without the confidence which both taxpayers and the Inland Revenue are able to place in the skill and integrity of members of the accountancy profession, the present vast taxation machinery would rapidly grind to a standstill.

Another sphere, one previously almost reserved to the lawyer, to which the accountant has recently been introduced is that of the legislation dealing with the valuation for estate duty of shares in private companies. It is perhaps interesting to note that in 1905 the History of Accounting and Accountants had suggested that " it is beginning to be recognised that this (the preparation of accounts and schedules in connection with Death Duties) is a kind of work more suited to the accountant."

New developments in costing, such as standard costs and systems of budgetary control, have also been stimulated and the mechanical aids necessary for the rapid production and collation of accounting information have become of increasing importance.

Professionally trained accountants have taken an ever more prominent place in the ranks of higher business executives and as company directors or financial advisers to boards of all types of concerns their services have been in great request. The latter development follows naturally from the earlier increase in the employment of professional accountants as whole-time officers of industrial concerns, but practising accountants are found in increasing numbers as directors of private and public companies.

Another field which since 1945 has absorbed a large number of accountants is public service, either directly under Government Departments or in the Nationalised Industries of Coal, Transport, Electricity and Gas and the National Health Service. During each of the two world wars large numbers of accountants were recruited to various Ministries for duties connected with war-time production and controls. The increasing concern of Governments with economic affairs and the growth of the Social

Services has, however, resulted in the retention in public service of a growing number of accountants. Professionally trained accountants are also frequently found in the service of Local Authorities.

These trends in the scope of professional activities have been reflected in changes in the examination syllabus, in the increased scope of the tutorial facilities available to students directly under the auspices of the Institute and in the provision of facilities for post-qualifying study through lectures and discussion groups. So much importance was attached to this last development that in 1949 a separate Director of Post-Qualifying Studies was appointed in Glasgow. The subjects of the post-qualifying lecture courses are mainly those of special interest to members in industry and commerce.

Over the past ten or fifteen years a notable feature of the official activity of the principal accounting bodies both in England and in the United States has been the preparation and issue of pronouncements on auditing procedure and on accounting principles. Apart from a memorandum on the Companies Act, 1948, issued by the Joint Committee of Councils, the Scottish chartered accountants did not issue any such official pronouncements prior to the amalgamation in 1951. The profession in Scotland is, however, keenly alive to the desirability of encouraging that study of theory of accounting which is usually designated "Accounting Research." Among the steps already taken by the unified Institute are the promotion of a prize essay competition on "The Future of Company Accounts" and the institution of a Summer School.

At the Sixth International Congress on Accounting, which was held in London in June 1952 and at which the Institute was one of the sponsoring bodies, the subjects of papers submitted reflected the main post-war pre-occupations of accountants throughout the world: the incidence of taxation, the problem of raising and retaining capital in face of changing money values and oppressive taxation, and the position of the accountant in industry, in practice, and in public service. Papers were submitted to the Congress by two members of the

Institute, Mr Ian W. Macdonald and Mr William S. Risk. As on the occasion of the previous Congress in London, a large party of visitors from abroad came to Scotland after the business sessions; on this occasion they were entertained by the Institute and the Scottish branches of other accountancy bodies.

Age brings experience and experience should bring wisdom, part of which is that age can still learn from youth. So in the international accounting field to which in the past it had made valuable contributions of men and ideas, the profession in Scotland has recently learned much from developments in younger countries. Some of the lessons are embodied in reports published by two teams which have visited the United States of America since the war, and which were led by Scottish chartered accountants—Mr Ian W. Morrow and Mr R. W. Parker. These reports dealing respectively with " Management Accounting " and " Cost Accounting and Productivity," illustrate some of the ways in which the accountancy profession can be of expanding service to industry.

To return from international questions to matters of more domestic interest to Scottish chartered accountants, the years since amalgamation have seen a few changes which call for comment. The administration of the affairs of an Institute of the size and standing of The Institute of Chartered Accountants of Scotland calls for a different type of organisation from that appropriate to the old independent Societies. A full-time Secretary and secretarial staff at headquarters in Edinburgh have taken the place of the practising members who gave such great service to the profession as part-time Secretaries of the three Societies, the General Examining Board, the Joint Committee of Councils and the Accountants' Publishing Co. Ltd. Fortunately this has not led to any loss of personal contact between officials and members, and the old friendly atmosphere still prevails.

One of those who did much to create that atmosphere by his unstinted service to his Institute and to the whole profession in Scotland has unfortunately passed to rest since 1951 when he resigned the last of the offices which he had filled with such acceptance for many years. Mr D. Norman Sloan succeeded his father as Secretary of the Glasgow Institute in 1909 and held that office for thirty years, when on his retirement he was appointed President for a term. He was also Secretary of the General Examining Board from 1916 till its extinction in 1951. A portrait of Mr Sloan presented to him on his retirement now hangs in the library at Glasgow where for so many years he came and went about the Institute's business, the object of universal respect and affection.

Among the duties taken over by the present Secretary and his staff is the editorial responsibility for THE ACCOUNTANTS' MAGAZINE. Although the Magazine has long been recognised as an official publication the editorial direction was left to "private enterprise" and for the long period of about thirty years the editorial chair was occupied by Professor A. G. Murray, C.A., to whose enthusiasm for the Magazine Scottish accountants owe a great debt. Through lean times and some few intervals of near prosperity, through war and peace, Professor Murray kept his beloved Magazine alive and so was able to hand over to the Institute when the time came a publication worthy to take its place as "The Journal of the Chartered Accountants of Scotland."

The final event to be noted with its evidence of fresh vitality in our centenarian Institute is the holding in 1953 of the first of what will certainly be a long and useful series of Summer Schools. The school was held in ideal surroundings in St Andrews at Scotland's oldest University. Papers worthy of the occasion were submitted and discussed, and all who were present derived from the School not only professional stimulus, but a remarkable sense of comradeship within the profession and between the practising and non-practising members.

So, as preparations proceed for the celebration of the centenary of organised accountancy in Scotland, our apprentice of 1904 can look back over fifty years of change, of development and of growth, throughout which the Scottish Societies have played a great part in the maintenance of the standards laid down for the profession by their founders. He may justly claim that they have been years of progress and may look confidently to a continuation of that progress by his successors.

CHAPTER V

THE PROFESSION TO-DAY

"A BALANCE SHEET always reminds me of a dead butterfly, pinned out with the dead, beautiful wings in formal symmetry on either side of the centre: all the meaning has gone out of the bustling transactions: they are transformed by some sterile accountants' magic into an unreal abstraction of balance. *Life* doesn't balance." So wrote Mr Paul Jennings of THE OBSERVER recently, and he expresses a feeling that is still shared by many, about the doings and the outlook of accountants. Those who have taken part in or followed the activities of the profession during the past thirty or forty years, however, would claim that it is increasingly concerned with living things and with the task of measuring and recording movement, and that accountants' magic, if they possess any, is being turned to constructive ends.

In the first part of this chapter it is proposed to examine the place in the business world of the accountant in public practice, and to show how that claim is justified.

The vast growth in the number of companies and increasing pressure by the Inland Revenue authorities for the production of audited accounts by private traders have combined to ensure that auditing is the predominant work of most practising accountants to-day. The auditor's report required by the Companies Act, 1929, referred only to the balance sheet, and responsibility for the profit and loss account was placed on the auditor merely by inference. Nevertheless this responsibility gradually came to be more generally accepted and the report prescribed by the Companies Act, 1948, placing as much emphasis on the statement of profit as on the balance sheet itself, was

MOORE CUP GOLF COMPETITION—GLENEAGLES, JUNE 10, 1947

THE COUNCIL OF THE INSTITUTE OF CHARTERED ACCOUNTANTS OF SCOTLAND, FEBRUARY 1954

Back Row (*Left to Right*): L. M. Davidson, T.D. (*Aberdeen Local Secretary*), J. J. Welch, C. G. M. Pearson, Graham A. Usher, M.B.E., T.D., J. Campbell Davies, M.C., T.D., S. E. Houstoun, M.A., Donald B. Grant (*Dundee Local Secretary*).

Middle Row: Charles D. Gairdner, J. G. Girdwood, C.B.E., Andrew R. Templeton, Norval M. Lindsay, P. M. Jackson, S. Gordon Y. Pool, Thomson S. Aikman, James A. Walker, C.B.E.

Front Row: E. H. V. McDougall (*Secretary of the Institute*), W. T. French, D.S.O., O.B.E., T.D., Robert Browning, M.A., LL.B., Sir Ian Bolton, Bt., O.B.E., L.L., J.P. (*Vice-President of the Institute*), John L. Somerville, F.R.S.E. (*President of the Institute*), Charles R. Munro, J. H. Johnston, Thomas Lister, M.A., William L. Davidson (*Glasgow Local Secretary*).

[*Absent*: R. G. S. Kirk and Andrew W. Mudie.]

recognised as bringing the legal obligation in this respect into line with current practice.

Of course, the modern auditor, like his predecessor, has to satisfy himself that the transactions of the business he is auditing have been properly recorded and that they have been duly authorised. This part of his task, however, is carried out to a much greater extent than formerly by observation and test of the system of internal control, so that a smaller proportion of the time of his staff is spent on monotonous routine checking; indeed some of the highly mechanised accounting systems now in common use may make that form of checking quite impracticable.

So far as auditing is concerned, therefore, there has been a marked shift from a static to a dynamic view.

This shift is even more evident in the tremendous increase in the calls for assistance and advice on taxation matters. This is not the place to discuss the pros and cons of a high level of taxation, but it is obvious that, when the Treasury is the senior partner in practically every commercial undertaking, the incidence of taxes in relation to business transactions demands the most carefully considered advice. Many firms of accountants have found it essential that one or more partners should concentrate on the study of income taxation and the larger firms usually have a department specialising in this branch. The problems which arise do not concern only the past: the tax implications of alternative methods of raising fresh capital, of the acquisition of a new business, of an overseas development, and of pension arrangements, to mention a few examples, all call for examination before wise decisions can be taken.

The practising accountant is concerned in these days with taxation not only on income but also on capital, and he has to be prepared to deal with problems arising in connection with estate duty. It might be thought that in this branch of his work, at any rate, it could scarcely be said that he was concerned with living matters. But, in the same way as in relation to income taxation, he must be able to advise his client during his lifetime as to the effects on ultimate liability for estate duty of the different courses of action that may be open. He will also frequently be called upon to negotiate with the Estate Duty Office in the valuation of shareholdings in private companies, of interests in partnerships and of other business assets.

The investigations which have to be made for the purpose of advising the seller or the buyer of a business or with a view to the signing of a prospectus certificate are, of course, directed to the verification of historical facts. The reporting accountant, nevertheless, must be conscious throughout that his client or the investing public is interested in these facts chiefly for the guidance they may give as to prospects. His paramount task, therefore, is to ensure that the facts are so stated that misleading conclusions will not be drawn, and to be satisfied that opinions expressed either by himself, in advising privately, or by others in an advertised prospectus, are justifiably related to actualities. Once again, he is concerned with the present and its bearing on the future, rather than with the past.

The responsibility of giving a prospectus certificate is one that few practitioners are inclined to underestimate, and it tends to reinforce the bias towards caution which is often regarded as a natural attribute of the Scot and an acquired characteristic of the chartered accountant. Mr Oliver Lyttelton told an audience a short time ago of a piece of advice that he would give to young aspirants for commercial honours: "Never sell a company on a chartered accountant's valuation, but if you can buy one upon it you will, in the long run, prosper." That may be taken by some as a compliment to the profession; others will sense a doubt as to the boasted objectivity of its judgments. It is clearly proper to ensure that any error should be in the direction of caution when the statement under examination is a representation by a seller, as in a prospectus. But in other cases, and especially in questions of valuation, which are continually presenting themselves to the accountant, his aim should be to give its true weight to every factor, favourable and unfavourable, and it is right that he should remember the difference between understatement of fact and prudence in action.

In problems of costing and management accounting generally the same trend as in auditing may be seen. No longer is a costing system regarded as fulfilling its purpose if it does no more than tell what products have cost in the past. It must give adequate information on which to base policy decisions and by which to judge day by day efficiency. For this the tools of budgets and standard costs have been developed, accompanied by the introduction of mechanical aids to shorten the interval between the event and the financial or statistical record of it.

The accountant of an earlier generation, who carried sovereigns in his pocket and took the gold standard for granted, was not much troubled by the problems raised by changes in the value of money, although he did, of course, sometimes meet the entry "loss on exchange." If one looks back to the period from 1918 to 1925 it now seems strange that there was so little discussion of the effects of a changing price level; this may have been because the phase of inflation ended within two years of the cessation of hostilities and was rapidly followed by a severe deflation. The omission has been amply made good in the past few years, and the debate continues between the advocates of historical cost and those of replacement cost. Where the Institute stands in this matter is shewn by the following statement on the subject issued by the Council in January, 1954:—

1. The "historical cost" basis which is so widely used in the measurement of profit has proved satisfactory when the value of money is steady or is changing slowly. On the other hand the limitations of this basis are evident and serious in periods of rapidly changing money values. The experience of the post-war years has demonstrated a clamant need for new conventions and methods which will compute the profit element in terms of current monetary costs as distinct from historical costs. Accountants in many parts of the world have been actively engaged in seeking appropriate solutions to this problem. In particular much attention has been given to the treatment of depreciation and to the valuation of stock, which are probably the two most important single factors involved in this question. While steady progress has been made in the development of new methods, the advance has so far been carried out almost entirely on the theoretical plane and little or no evidence is yet available

of the effectiveness of new techniques applied over a period to practical cases. Since the development is still at the theoretical stage it is not surprising that considerable divergence of views prevails amongst accountants as to the new conventions which will best meet both inflationary and deflationary movements.

2. The Council's view is that until some of these divergences have been resolved on the basis of practical experience it is clearly inappropriate for a professional body to advocate to its members the adoption of any particular method. On the other hand the Council holds the view that the accountancy bodies, singly and collectively, should now urge their members to take an active part in promoting the practical application of new conventions, and should give collective support where possible to practical experiments and research.

3. In so far as the position of an Auditor is concerned, the Council is of opinion that what constitutes " a true and fair view " of the state of the affairs of a company and of the profit for a stated period must always be a matter for decision in relation to the facts of a particular case, but that there is no reason in principle why an auditor should qualify his report on accounts by reason only of some disclosed departure from the basis of " historical cost."

4. The Council would welcome experiments by individual undertakings which have as their objective the presentation of accounts in which all items in the trading and profit and loss account are expressed in pounds sterling of the same purchasing power. The problem arises not only in the presentation of the results of each year or other financial period, but also in the presentation of the results for a number of financial periods, particularly where it is desired to establish trends. The desirability of showing in the balance sheet the capital employed expressed in pounds sterling of the same money value also merits consideration. The importance of the problem varies as between one undertaking and another. What can or might be done should only be decided after very careful consideration of the facts of each particular case. Where there is a departure from the basis of " historical cost " (whether in the body of the financial accounts or by way of supplementary figures or statements) what has been done and the basis adopted should be clearly shown.

5. It is considered that in the field of Management Accounting it is eminently desirable, in many cases, that account should be taken of changing money values. Failure to do so in times of progressive inflation may well create a complacent attitude not in the best interest of any undertaking as a continuing concern. In Management Accounting many statements are prepared only for the guidance of those engaged in the day to day administration of the undertaking and the planning of its future activities. The values to be used in these cases should be those which will most realistically reflect the outcome of the trading operations of the undertaking and its financial stability.

If a book on similar lines to this one is produced for the Institute's 150th birthday, its readers may be amused by the somewhat tentative suggestions set out above—or will they still be debating the issues involved?

The contacts of the practising accountant with business enterprise are not confined to his work as auditor, taxation adviser, investigator, and consultant on accounting systems. He is frequently called upon to take part in negotiations on behalf of his clients and he may be retained as financial adviser. The help that he can give in these capacities is somewhat analogous to the part of an advocate in litigation: he must, in the main, rely on the technical knowledge and skill of the experts, but he should be able to test their judgments against the background of a more general and varied experience. The fact that accountants have been judged successful in such matters has led to a great increase in the number appointed to boards of directors, not only of insurance offices, investment trusts, banks and other financial concerns, but of commercial and industrial companies as well. Many, indeed, are to be found in high executive positions, but that is a topic for another chapter.

Mention should also be made of work done for trade associations and other groups. If it is desired to compile statistics or to ascertain costs for a whole industry or a particular section of an industry, returns can be made confidentially by the various undertakings concerned to a firm of accountants, for examination, analysis or aggregation as may be required. The needs of Government Departments during and since the Second World War led to a considerable extension of costing and statistical work of this kind, and in many cases the information made available has been proved valuable to the industry as a whole, as well as to the department. The accountants concerned have also frequently been called upon to take part in price negotiations between industrial groups and Government Departments.

The long period of inflation which this country has experienced and the nature of many of the Government controls imposed during and after the Second World War have both tended to make business failures uncommon, and in consequence for the past fifteen years bankruptcies, liquidations and (in England) receiverships have formed a much less important part of an accountant's work than at any previous time. No one would wish to see either a return of unemployment or a recrudescence of bad debts. If, however, inflation is checked and trade and industry become fully competitive once more, some of the less efficient concerns will almost certainly be casualties, and it must be expected that the profession will again be concerned with windings-up and reconstructions. Although a company may be forced into liquidation, the business itself is not necessarily dead. The failure may be due to a permanent change in demand, or an inherently bad location, or the competition of a substitute that is produced at lower cost ; in such cases there is probably no chance of salvation. On the other hand it may be caused by shortage of capital, a sudden movement in the price of a raw material, the failure of an important customer, or by general bad management ; and the liquidator may be able even when the company is *in extremis* to rescue the undertaking by a reconstruction scheme.

There is another rôle in which the professional accountant in public practice has a useful function to perform and that is as an expert witness before the Courts in criminal trials or civil cases. It is a type of work for which not all accountants are suited, but it involves often a high public duty, and many chartered accountants have given valuable service in this capacity. The work is arduous and exacting ; it requires in the first place a keen intelligence and an ability to grasp the details of a complicated case, combined with a clear knowledge of the principles of law involved. Thereafter there must be a patient and laborious examination, occupying possibly a long period, of numerous books and documents, which of itself will require a knowledge not only of accountancy but of customs of trade and kindred matters. All this must then be condensed into a report which will form the basis of the accountant's evidence ; and lastly there is the ordeal of examination and cross-examination in Court when he must have the whole case at his finger-tips and where hesitation in replying to a single question may have the worst results. It is a sphere in which assistants can be used only to a limited extent and where the accountant must himself accept the necessity for many hours of concentrated work. The accountancy profession has in the past produced many who were of high eminence in this rôle, and it continues to do so.

What has been written above relates most directly to the work to be found in the office of a firm carrying on a varied practice in a large city, but if some allowance is made for difference in scale it is equally true of those practising in the smaller centres, because the problems of the client, whether a large manufacturing company or a modest "one-man" business, are similar in their fundamentals. The accountants practising in the smaller towns have a most useful contribution to make to the profession. Their work brings them into direct personal contact with many clients—tradesmen, farmers, fishermen, and others—who often have little knowledge of the formalities of business and who seek the advice of their accountant on a wide range of problems. In auditing the books and preparing the accounts of these clients and in adjusting their affairs with the Inland Revenue, the accountant has responsibilities to his clients, his profession and the public authorities which will often call for the practical application of business ethics as well as of accountancy skills, and for an entirely objective approach. There have been great improvements in the standard of book-keeping and accounts in smaller businesses during the last fifty years, although much may yet remain to be done. For such improvements as have been achieved, the accountancy profession is largely to be thanked, and its work continues. Moreover farmers and fishermen—to name only two occupations—have business problems to face which require specialised knowledge on the part of their accountants; their needs are understood and met by a section of the profession which performs a useful public service in an atmosphere sometimes very different from that of professional practice in the larger cities.

Whether the accountant of to-day, therefore, is acting as auditor, as consultant on taxation, on costing, or on more general problems, or even if he is called in to secure what is possible for creditors, and whether he be in large practice or small or in town or country, his function is far removed from that of the collector of specimens, however beautiful and skilfully mounted, in which life and movement have been destroyed.

Scottish accountants have long had close connections with the law. Notwithstanding the fact that the two professions are competing to some extent in the fields of trust administration and taxation, it is recognised by both that, especially as regards taxation, there is ample scope for co-operation between them ; likewise in company matters, insolvency work and Court remits their respective spheres are distinct, and accountants would agree that they derive much pleasure, considerable mental stimulus and some profit from association with their legal brethren.

Reference has already been made to the increasing prominence of valuation problems in the work of an accountant to-day. These problems may bring him into contact with valuators, engineers and actuaries, and the accountant must understand something of their techniques, if he is to obtain full advantage of the knowledge and skill of these other professions.

In the sphere of management accountancy there are obvious opportunities for co-operation with specialists in other aspects of management ; production planning, motion study and market research are examples that come immediately to mind. To accountants, at any rate, it would appear that their clients are likely to be best served by seeking help in their management accounting problems from their accountants, and guidance in the physical and psychological problems of manufacturing and selling from specialists in management.

The syllabus for apprentices includes a course in economics and an examination in the elements of statistical methods. It could not be claimed that a deep study of these subjects is demanded, but their inclusion in the course should at least give the young accountant some idea of what the facts with which he had to deal mean to the economist, and the statistician. It seems almost certain that accountants, statisticians and economists will learn to work more closely with each other than in the past, and their co-operation should produce results which will be of help to business undertakings as well as furthering the cause of science.

The Second World War made many demands on the profession, which have been discussed in Chapter IV, and they could not have been met without close co-operation among the principal bodies of accountants. Their representatives sat on many occasions on joint committees and a more intimate and friendly association was established than had existed before; since the end of the war the joint committees—or some of them—and the friendly association have both continued. In particular Scottish chartered accountants would like to acknowledge the cordiality of their relations with The Institute of Chartered Accountants in England and Wales, who not only tolerate the invasion of England by 1,700 Scotsmen, but extend to them the hospitality of their Hall and Library in Moorgate Place and, in many cases, take them into partnership.

At this point something should be said of the activities of the Scottish Institute at the present time.

The part which a professional body such as the Institute plays in the life of the profession has become much more comprehensive during the last hundred years. To-day the basic functions of the Institute are not dissimilar from when it was founded—maintaining proper standards of education and training to be required of those seeking to become members, keeping a register of members, ensuring the observance of proper professional etiquette and discipline, providing libraries and other facilities for members' use and generally working to maintain and enhance the standard of the profession and the interests of its members. But the scope of the Institute's activities under these heads has grown rapidly with the passing of the years.

The work of the Institute is touched upon throughout this book, but it may be convenient to summarise here what the Institute of to-day is seeking to do and how it is going about its task. This can perhaps be done most easily by viewing the Institute through the eyes of one who seeks to join it.

First, our intending candidate will study a booklet summarising the Rules for admission of members and the syllabus of examinations. He will then soon realise that he should at the earliest moment consult one of the Institute's Directors of Studies for advice as to his course of study for the profession; that he must at the outset produce to the Institute evidence of a high standard of general education; that he must register with the Institute an indenture of apprenticeship with a member in practice; that during apprenticeship he may be paid a salary in accordance with a scale recommended by the Institute; that under arrangements made by the Institute with the Ministry of Labour and National Service he may be entitled during his apprenticeship to deferment of call-up for National Service; that he must attend certain University classes prescribed by the Institute; that he should also attend tutorial classes provided by the Institute; that he should belong to a Students' Society, largely financed by the Institute; that he will have the use of the Institute's Libraries from which he may borrow books; that he must pass the examinations which the Institute conducts; that he must register with the Institute the discharge of his indenture when it is completed; and after all this he may apply to the Institute for admission as a member.

On admission, our new member's contacts with the Institute continue. Each year he pays an annual subscription, the rate of which varies according to whether he is in practice or not or is in the United Kingdom or elsewhere; he is under a duty to tell the Institute of any change in his address; his name appears in the Official Directory which the Institute publishes; he may make use of the appointment registers which the Institute maintains; he continues to have the right to use the Institute's buildings in Edinburgh and Glasgow, and to borrow books from the Institute's libraries in Glasgow, Edinburgh, and Aberdeen—by post from the Glasgow Library if he does not live in that city; he can continue to belong to a Students' Society; he may join one or more of the Institute's discussion groups on professional subjects; he may attend the Institute's Summer School; and he may also take part in the Moore Cup Golf Competition and the other social gatherings which the Institute organises from time to time.

These are the member's direct contacts with the Institute, but there are other more indirect benefits which he derives from his membership. First, the Institute watches over matters of professional etiquette and discipline: this branch of the Institute's work is small in volume but great in importance, as upon its proper performance depends the maintenance of the high standards required of members of the Institute upon which members themselves, as well as the general public, are entitled to rely. Secondly, the Institute plays its part in protecting and advancing the interests of the accountancy profession as a whole and of Scottish chartered accountants in particular: it is safe to say that at each of its monthly meetings the Council has some subject of this kind to consider, whether it be the form of the audit clause in some new legislation or the effect upon members of the Institute of some new development in the accountancy profession overseas, or some problem which has arisen with some other profession on the debatable ground near the borders of the accountant's field of activity, or the making of recommendations as to the basis of professional charges. Thirdly, as a responsible professional body, the Institute submits views to Royal Commissions, Departmental Committees and Government Departments on subjects with which accountants are concerned. In these days, when "the welfare State" shows such a close interest in almost everything that almost everyone does, this last part of the work is of very great importance, as unless those who can speak from practical experience are prepared to offer their views in good time the formulation of sound policy and administration is much impeded. Our member may not be able to lay his hand on his pocket and say that he can value these branches of the Institute's work by any precise number of guineas or pounds that have thereby accrued to him personally: nevertheless, if he reads of these matters in the

Council's Annual Report and in THE ACCOUNTANTS' MAGAZINE he may feel that whether he is in practice or not he derives not only prestige and standing but also financial benefit by being a member of a professional body which has a not unimportant place in affairs.

From this brief sketch of the Institute's work for members and apprentices it will be realised that the activities of the Institute do not merely happen, but that they involve much forethought and planning, an effective administrative organisation and the expenditure of money. It was, indeed, with this in mind that the amalgamation of the three Societies of Scottish Chartered Accountants was brought about in 1951.

The affairs of the Institute are now governed by a Council consisting of the President, the Vice-President and twenty-one ordinary members: the members of the Council are supported by many other members of the Institute who serve on numerous Standing and Special Committees to which important parts of the work are decentralised. Under this system the Council devotes itself to the broader questions of policy, and the consideration of other questions arising in the conduct of the Institute's business is undertaken by Committees such as the Finance and General Purposes Committee, the Examining Board, the Local Committees, the Tutorial Classes Committees, the Discipline Committee and the Taxation Committee. The Council is required by the Institute's Rules to include members practising in Scotland, members practising elsewhere in the United Kingdom and members not in practice. Under existing arrangements members of the Council are drawn from Edinburgh, Glasgow, Aberdeen, Dundee and London, and there are also three other members from other parts of Scotland—at present Perth, Dumfries and Elgin. There are two members not in practice.

The whole-time staff consists of a Secretary, two Assistant Secretaries, a Librarian and supporting staff at the headquarters in Edinburgh, and a Librarian and supporting staff in Glasgow. In addition there are practising members who act as Local

Secretaries of the Institute in Glasgow, Aberdeen, Dundee, Inverness and London. In all these places, except Inverness, the Institute provides tutorial classes which are organised by Directors of Studies, and conducted by Lecturers, Assistant Lecturers and Tutors under the direction of Tutorial Classes Committees: these act on a part-time basis and the great majority of them are members of the Institute. In Glasgow and Aberdeen the Local Committees have appointed practising members of the Institute to act as Auditors of Fees and to dispose of any difficulties or disputes which may arise about members' professional charges.

The membership of the Institute at March 31, 1954, was 5,608; as appears from the following table (which may be compared with that for 1904 given on page 47) just over half of these were in Scotland, almost a third were in England, Wales and Northern Ireland, and the remainder, slightly over a sixth, were abroad:—

Scotland	2,924
England and Northern Ireland	1,727
British Commonwealth	647
United States of America	114
Other countries abroad	196

The proportions in practice, employed in professional offices and employed in industry, vary greatly from place to place; while 33 per cent of the members in Scotland are in practice, the corresponding percentages elsewhere in the United Kingdom and abroad are 12 and 22 respectively.

The distribution of members overseas is not without interest. Apart from the United Kingdom, they are to be found in seventy-one countries. As one might expect, there are many members in such great cities as Johannesburg, where there are 57, Montreal (56), Calcutta (44) and New York City (43): these "outposts" may appear small when compared with the main groups of members in the United Kingdom—Glasgow (1,210), London (934) and Edinburgh (586)—but they are larger than those in many of the other cities and towns here at home. But not only are members to be found in the great cities overseas : the geographical list of the distribution of members which appears in the Institute's Directory conjures up some romantic pictures for the dreamer and sets an interesting test of general knowledge for the "quiz" specialist. Honiara (British Solomon Islands), Carapichaima (British West Indies), Suva (Fiji Islands), Aliartos (Greece), Lihue (Territory of Hawaii), Madura (India), Curepipe (Mauritius), Enugu (Nigeria), Nzara (Sudan) and Izmir (Turkey) are a few of the places where Scottish chartered accountants are to be found : perhaps not everyone could pin-point more than two of these on the map or would think of them as places where auditing, cost accounting, taxation and business management were likely to be subjects of keen interest and—more than that—provide remunerative employment.

The profession has been accustomed, over a long period of rapid expansion, to a situation in which a high proportion of the younger members only remain in professional employment for a few years. During these years valuable experience should be gained and the ability to accept responsibility should develop. But unless the assistant is promoted to be a managing clerk, or secures a partnership, the scope for advancement in a professional office is limited, although there is still room for a man of courage and initiative to " put up his plate " and found a new accountancy practice of his own.

So long as the demands of industry and commerce for chartered accountants continue to grow, there will normally be little difficulty in finding senior posts of adequate interest and responsibility for those who do not move into business ; indeed at present the position rather is that the pull of business is so strong that it is not easy to retain in practice as many of the abler men as could be wished.

A time may come, however, when the requirements of industry will cease to expand except in proportion to the growth of industry itself, and vacancies will then be broadly limited to those created by deaths and retirements. It is possible, of course, that some new and at present unforeseeable call for chartered accountants will develop, but, unless that should happen, a stage would be reached where the prospect before the new member of the Institute would have altered materially. A larger proportion of the profession would of necessity be looking for a permanent career, whether as principal or as assistant, in public practice, and the possibility of attracting entrants of the right quality would come once more to depend on there being professional openings which would be adequately rewarding not only as regards remuneration but also in the continuing interest of the work. Practising members would have to adapt themselves to the altered conditions, and a change in the normal staffing of professional offices might well follow : an increase in the number of assistants having the status of managing clerk, a reduction in the use of qualified assistants on individual audits and greater employment of clerical staff trained in auditing procedure.

Such a change would be a gradual one, and it is not suggested that any violent disturbance of the accepted order is likely to overtake the profession in the near future : the question is one of evolution rather than revolution, and a constant watch must be kept so as to ensure that the Institute and its members can adapt themselves to the needs of the time as and when those needs change. As this book has shewn, the profession has not been slow to adapt itself in the past and it remains vigorous and youthful, even if it can no longer claim to be young. In 1904, as mentioned in an earlier chapter, there were grave fears that the profession was overstocked and the future appeared to be viewed with some gloom. The fifty years that ensued brought with them many trials, troubles, and indeed horrors, but the accountancy profession continued to go on from strength to strength. Without being complacent, therefore, one may be permitted to look to the future with reasonable confidence.

The tasks of an accountant in practice have steadily increased in complexity with the enlarging scale and growing complication of business affairs, and he may sometimes feel that he has become the slave of Acts of Parliament and regulations of all kinds. But the profession still affords scope for the ability to examine and present facts objectively, to analyse a problem, and to discover the principle underlying a mass of detail, and for the exercise of individual judgment. So long as it does this, there is every reason to feel assured that it will continue to offer a career giving not only material but intellectual reward and the satisfaction of useful service rendered.

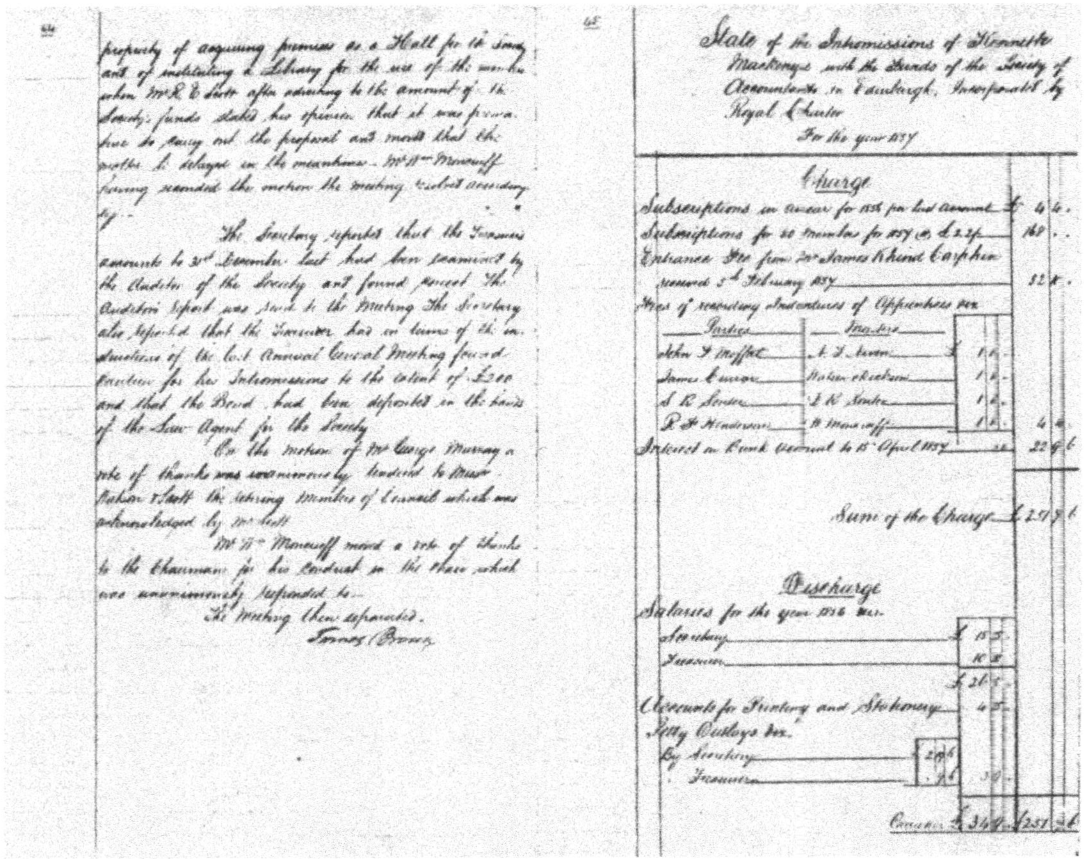

EXCERPT FROM THE FIRST MINUTE BOOK OF THE SOCIETY OF ACCOUNTANTS IN EDINBURGH

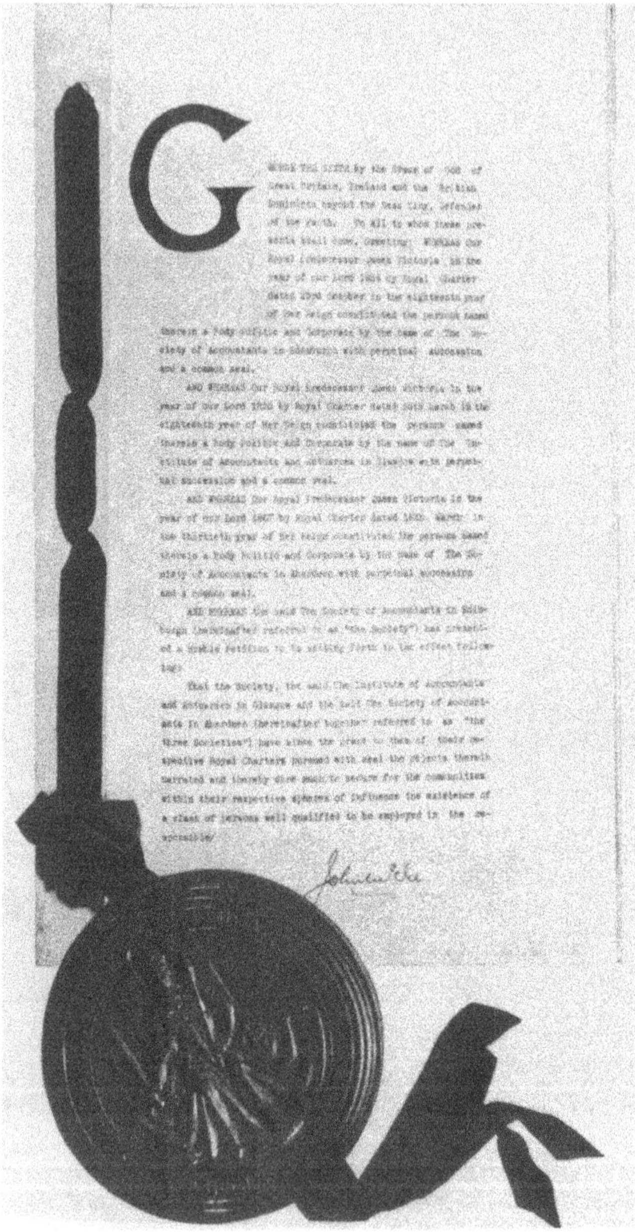

THE SUPPLEMENTARY ROYAL CHARTER OF 1951

CHAPTER VI

THE CHARTERED ACCOUNTANT IN INDUSTRY

THE important place occupied by chartered accountants in industry and commerce at the present time merits a special chapter in this book. Historically there can be no doubt that the first accountants were employed in this sphere many centuries ago, since the need to have business accurately recorded was probably first felt as soon as the control of production passed out of the hands of the individual craftsman. As the business of the merchant traders developed, the practice of recording transactions grew; and when the settlement of transactions by coin, and later by paper, became established, the need for keeping accurate accounts became paramount. All this took place a long time before there was any conception of a professional audit or of the employment of a practising accountant as these terms are understood to-day.

Reference has been made in an earlier chapter to the Scottish accountants employed by the Darien Company, formed in 1696, and by the numerous banks which sprang into existence during the next two centuries. Various important positions such as Accountant-General to the Scottish Board of Excise and Accountant to the General Post Office in Scotland were held by men who were eminent accountants in their day. As has also been related, accountants were employed by the early life assurance societies and many of these rose to the position of manager.

When the Scottish Chartered Societies were formed a century ago, their intention in their respective cities was to incorporate in one body the accountants in public practice. Since then the profession has developed in many directions which were never contemplated by its founders, but these developments were of slow growth to begin with and the full-time employment of qualified accountants by industry on anything like a large scale is a twentieth-century phenomenon. Indeed until the First World War there were still comparatively few qualified accountants in industry. The development which followed may not have been one which the profession consciously sought. It was however due to the operation of economic law: industry saw the advantages to itself of enlisting trained accountants, and the practising side of the profession could not offer rewards adequate to retain them all. In the period of readjustment that ensued there were not wanting those who regarded accountants transferring into industry as lost sheep, but the lost sheep in their turn declared that the professional pastures did not suit them and in any event could not provide sustenance for all. Now, however, a high mutual respect exists between members of the Institute in both branches of the profession and relationships are established on a happy basis.

There are unfortunately not sufficient data available to provide accurate figures of the number of Scottish accountants who have left public practice for industry, but from a perusal of the Official Directories it is probably safe to say that when the Scottish Societies celebrated their fiftieth anniversary in 1904/5 not more than 100 members were engaged in industry: it is estimated that over 2,800 members are so engaged to-day. This influx of Scottish accountants into industry is not confined to the home country, and for anyone who is travel-minded there is an air of romance surrounding many of the names of the lands to which members of the Institute have penetrated. In the Americas, from Canada in the north to Chile in the south, from Brazil in the east to California in the west; in North Africa, Central Africa, South Africa; in the East Indies, the West Indies and in many of the outlying parts of the British Commonwealth we find them at work. The Scottish race have long been noted for seeking their fortunes in distant lands and in this respect the Scottish accountant has been true to tradition. In all, nearly 1,000 members, many of whom are directly employed by industry, are to-day residing in 71 countries abroad.

Fifty years ago Richard Brown wrote in his HISTORY OF ACCOUNTING AND ACCOUNTANTS: "The employment of accountants as book-keepers is no doubt one of the humbler walks of the profession." It is very evident that the last half-century has been notable not only for the growth in numbers of accountants in industry but also for the manner in which the functions of the accountants so employed have extended far beyond those of the humble book-keeper. Many factors have combined to set the conditions which have brought about this development. The most important among them have been the growth of joint stock enterprise, and, more recently, the growth of groups of companies and the increasing complexity of financial structure; competition in its widest sense, including the inventiveness of the age and technological advancement; the impact of two world wars; high taxation; the increasing participation of the Government in the affairs of the producing and trading community; and the growing recognition of the contribution which accountants can bring to the modern concepts of the technique of management. All these factors have given rise to a much greater cost-consciousness in industry and have imposed requirements of exactitude in the conduct of business affairs far removed from the old "rule of thumb" methods. They have also led perforce to the gradual replacement of direct and personal management by control through statistical and accounting information.

Much as this helps to explain industry's ever-increasing need for specialists in accounting and the extending scope of the accountant's activities, it does not immediately explain the accountant's ability to occupy successfully high positions in the company hierarchy. To-day professional accountants are to be found holding the appointment of chairman, managing director, director, general manager, departmental manager, company secretary, comptroller, treasurer, chief accountant and other similar posts. Nor are such appointments confined to any particular branch of industry for, as the Institute's Directory shows, Scottish accountants control or hold high positions in some of the leading companies in such diverse industries as ship-owning, iron and steel, shipbuilding and engineering, textiles, chemicals, food stuffs, distilling and newspapers. What then are the professional accountant's particular qualities that industry finds so useful ?

The accountant who enters industry as a member of one of the professional bodies which require a period of training under apprenticeship or articles starts off with an initial advantage. One of the chief merits of the apprenticeship system is that it not only gives a sound training in the fundamental principles of accounting and allied subjects but also provides for a wide variety of practical experience. From this training the accountant acquires an objective approach, learns impartiality and develops a disciplined mind ; he becomes able to sift information and to distinguish between facts which are relevant and those which are not ; he gains experience in many companies and of many business systems and carries responsibility at a comparatively early age ; he achieves a facility with figures and is able to interpret them. By his training and experience the accountant is able to comprehend the whole range of industrial processes—the design, production, buying, selling and financial aspects. Thus he can advise and often enlarge upon or modify the opinions of the industrial specialists ; for often it is only when the facts are expressed in figures and in terms of money that their commercial significance is fully appreciated. To these qualities the Scottish chartered accountant may perhaps claim, in addition, the special attributes and characteristics of his race. His conservative outlook, in the business and financial sense, his native caution and shrewdness, and a consciousness from an early age of the need for hard and solid work, all equip him well for the business field.

The accountant's first appointment in industry is generally in the accountancy department or in the secretary's office and it may well be that some time elapses before he feels that his work is of value to his employers. The way in which the affairs of the firm are handled and the basic technical processes have to be learned. He must guard himself against any previous tendency to regard the annual accounts as the be-all and the end-all of the accounting function and must apply his knowledge of accounting in a much wider field. Thus, although he cannot expect to attain at once all the qualities demanded of an industrial accountant, his professional training is such that he should be able quickly to broaden his knowledge to meet the requirements of his new sphere of activity.

It has been suggested by some critics that what are claimed as virtues become vices when the accountant is in an executive position. They hold that his training is apt to make him too cautious, too slow, too ready to say " no " rather than " yes " ; that he is liable to be overcome by events before he is finished weighing up the considerations ; that he is better at giving several reasons why a scheme will not work than at making one constructive suggestion for making it work. There may be an element of truth in these criticisms in cases where these virtues are carried to excess, but it may fairly be said that the men to whom they are justly applied are not only bad executives but also bad accountants. As Mr J. K. Knight [1] has put it, " The advantage that a well-trained professional accountant has lies in the quickness of mind and flexibility that result from being frequently confronted with unfamiliar situations which have to be understood and acted upon quickly."

The importance of this advantage is emphasised if we look more closely at the accountant's rôle in industry. From the above list of positions which accountants hold, it will be seen that their appointments fall into two broad categories :—

(1) The secretary, comptroller, chief accountant or cost accountant, in which capacities the accountant is called upon to provide the financial information which management needs in making policy decisions and to show the effect of these decisions :

(2) The director or financial adviser, in which capacity he shares the responsibility for making policy decisions.

How different from the work of the humble book-keeper is the rôle of the accountant as an executive officer in industry

[1] "Accountant in Industry," by Jasper K. Knight : PROGRESS, Spring 1952.

to-day. The success of a business largely depends on judgment backed by experience; and to exercise this judgment in present-day conditions boards and managements need detailed and comprehensive information as to the probable return and savings which would be effected by any scheme under consideration. Here the comptroller or accounting officer is best fitted to examine and provide such information, but it is essential that this should be expressed in easily understandable terms.

In fulfilling this function the accountant's aims are speed, reliability, relevance and comprehensiveness. The extent to which these sometimes conflicting elements can be reconciled is a measure of the success of the accountant's service and calls for a highly developed sense of judgment allied to an adequate technical ability. But it also demands a well-organised office procedure so that all relevant information is easily and quickly available—with all that this entails in the way of suitably adapted office machinery and systems, and efficient departmental management.

In the modern company the accountancy department reflects these needs. Besides the work connected with the annual accounts, taxation and internal audit—with which practising accountants are familiar—there are the functions of costing, statistics, finance and organisation and methods, which are the tools of present-day management accounting. Here the controlling instrument, the combination of standard costs and budgetary control, operates within the framework of a system of accounts so integrated that the attention of management is quickly directed to divergent factors. In this connection it is important to remember that in its work the relationships which the accountancy department establishes with other departments, as well as the degree of harmonious co-operation that it can develop among departments, is vital to the efficiency of the whole enterprise.

Largely as a result of the Second World War, the problems which to-day beset business are more varied and complex than usual and, as finance must enter into nearly all questions of policy, the chartered accountant, in his capacity as director or financial adviser, will find full scope for the exercise of these qualities which his earlier training has developed.

On the production side the advance in science and production methods and the drive to increase this country's export trade in the face of ever-increasing world competition raise questions of reconstruction and modernisation of plant and expansion of productive capacity. Allied to these is the need to expand the sales organisation, which may call for the formation of subsidiary companies abroad and a close study of the effect of Government restrictions on quotas and currencies in foreign markets.

Closely connected with these problems is the question of the provision of adequate working capital. Owing to the change in the value of money, with a corresponding increase in the monetary value of stocks and debtors, the incidence of purchase tax and the heavy burden of taxation, many businesses are finding themselves short of working capital for their normal requirements. When, in addition, they are called upon to finance the capital expenditure needed for new plant and increased production, the problem becomes more acute and requires a high degree of financial skill in searching for and arriving at the best solution.

The financial institutions, such as banks, insurance companies and investment trusts, are to-day increasingly becoming the source from which industry's capital requirements are met and they have to face these same problems from a different angle. Many of these financial houses have chartered accountants on their boards. It is also significant to note that two of the largest banks in Scotland have appointed Scottish chartered accountants to the important post of general manager.

The fall in the purchasing power of money has created other problems such as the proper accounting valuation of physical assets, the provision of reserves for the replacement of assets at greatly increased costs, and the basis on which to calculate real production costs in the light of these and other inflationary factors.

In dealing with these problems there is unique value in the accountant's familiarity with the broad range of company operations, the ways in which the necessary financial information can be marshalled and presented, and the interpretation of the figures provided. His greatest asset, however, is that facility for objective judgment, based on knowledge, which his training and wide experience provide.

The importance of this contribution to policy-making is well illustrated by the remark made by the holder of "a distinguished position in the City of London"—not an accountant—to Mr K. A. E. Moore, F.C.A., and quoted by him at a meeting of The Institute of Chartered Accountants in England and Wales:[1] "In my earlier years I often had experience of boards coming to wrong decisions because they had only half the story before them. Nowadays I always see to it that there is a chartered accountant on all my boards, not because he is necessarily wiser than any other person of experience in considering matters of policy, but because a chartered accountant, by his training, seems to have a flair for ensuring that all the material facts and considerations are before a board when they are making up their minds on an important matter with a financial angle to it."

Mention should also be made of the service which the profession can give to industry through the medium of trade associations. Simultaneously with the growth of the trades union movement there came into existence federations and associations of employers which negotiate with the unions on questions relating to wages and labour conditions. In more recent years trade associations have been formed to deal with commercial affairs in a wider sphere, and many industries have learned to appreciate the value of such associations in assisting and protecting the interests of their members. The Government also have not been slow to appreciate the advantages of dealing with one body which can speak for the whole industry; and not only have the Government encouraged the formation

[1] "The Accountant as Financial Adviser," a paper read by K. A. E. Moore, F.C.A., at the 1953 Autumnal Meeting of the English Institute.

of such associations but they have in some instances been instrumental in bringing them into being.

The functions of the trade associations vary according to the needs of the particular industry, but generally their aims are to protect the members against unfair competition, to encourage the installation of adequate costing systems, to collect statistical information on various matters affecting the industry and to interpret the figures so collected, to assist and encourage trade with foreign countries, to negotiate with the Government on behalf of the industry on questions such as controls, quotas, maximum prices, terms of government contracts and other relevant matters, to advise the members on all new legislation affecting the industry and to present the views of industry to the Government on questions of taxation and other kindred subjects. The chartered accountant is well qualified by his training to conduct the affairs of trade associations and to organise and control the secretariat necessary to carry out their functions. That this has been recognised is evidenced by the number of professional accountants who hold such posts as director or secretary in these organisations.

It is clear from the trend of the past hundred years, and particularly from the more rapid course of events in the last half-century, that further developments may be expected in the functions which the accountant in industry performs and in the techniques he employs. Economic conditions to-day demand that industry and trade be conducted in the most efficient and scientific manner. Since modern control systems and financial data are essential features of such methods and are basic to many aspects of the constructive approach to management, it is apparent that this vital new field for the accountant's art has yet to be fully exploited. Perhaps, as Mr David Solomons has suggested,[1] there will be a progressive simplification of procedure, with statistical sampling methods reducing the volume of work in the accounts department; and, as more attention is paid to the positive use of costing

[1] "Costing Techniques—Their Effect on Management Practice and Policy," by David Solomons: THE MANAGER, November 1953.

information by management, the accountant may find need of a greater knowledge of statistical methods; perhaps, too, there can be expected a much greater application of costing methods to the distribution function, so that firms can analyse distribution costs between products, or between methods of distribution, or between types of customer and so on. No doubt increasing attention will also have to be paid in future to the use of capital resources and the provision and reorganisation of capital.

Until recent years the Societies of Scottish chartered accountants, in accordance with their initial purpose, devoted most of their time and resources to fostering the work of their members as public accountants. The rapid growth in the number of accountants in industry and the widening scope of their functions were bound, however, to have an impact on the activities of the professional bodies. There are of course marked differences between the duties of industrial and practising accountants, but in many instances, such as the form in which the financial accounts are presented, taxation, and the installation and improvement of accounting systems, their duties merge and a close liaison is essential.

This interdependence of accountants in public practice and in industry was recognised some time ago by the Scottish chartered bodies when their non-practising members were given representation on their Councils. The unified Institute has continued the same practice and two seats on the Council have been allotted to members who are not in practice. A Non-practising Members' Committee was also formed some years ago in Glasgow to give accountants in industry an opportunity of discussing matters of common interest and of expressing their views to the Council.

The Institute has also not been unmindful of the need to keep its facilities for training in line with new requirements and the Council has reviewed, from time to time, the examination syllabus and the curriculum of the tutorial classes held under its auspices. For example, in the classes provided in three of the Scottish Universities and elsewhere, in which accounting and business methods in all branches affecting the accountant's work are taught, more emphasis has been placed on the teaching of such subjects as costing, business statistics and budgetary control. These classes, which are compulsory, are taken by the apprentice before presenting himself for the final examination of the Institute.

The question of the examination and training of apprentices is at the moment being considered anew by a Special Committee of the Institute. The Committee will, no doubt, review amongst other matters the extent to which the present system of apprenticeship and tuition meets the needs of those members of the profession who intend to make their career in industry. The present curriculum covers a wide variety of subjects and demands a high degree of concentration on the part of the student, both as regards his work in the classroom and in its practical application. Should the number of subjects covered by the present course of study be increased to any appreciable extent, there would be a danger of over-burdening the apprentice so that his present sound training in the fundamentals of accountancy would suffer.

To meet these conditions the Institute has now provided in Glasgow a course of lectures in Management and Works Accounting for members of the Institute who are desirous of taking up commercial careers. The lectures are given by specialists and cover the whole range of costing and business administration with which an accountant in industry has to deal. The course, which has proved very popular, is open not only to members but also to students who have passed the final examination. In addition to the lectures, discussion groups have been formed to enable members to exchange views on practical problems arising in their day to day work in industry. The groups are fulfilling an important function and are of considerable benefit especially to the younger members of the profession. These facilities for lectures and discussion would appear to provide a solution to the problem of special training, and, as the subject-matter of the lectures can easily be adjusted or extended as occasion requires, the changes which are taking place in accounting technique to-day can be adequately met.

The suggestion has been made from time to time that the apprentice chartered accountant might be seconded to an industrial firm for a period during the course of his training. There are undoubted attractions in this suggestion from the point of view of practical training, but the two main objections are that it is doubtful if the apprentice can afford the time from his normal basic training in a professional office and the practical difficulty of finding sufficient industrial companies which would be prepared to assist in carrying out the scheme. If a young man went into industry for a short period after passing his final examination and simultaneously took the special course of lectures mentioned above, he would be in a much better position to receive the maximum benefit from this training, which would be of great value to him whether he went into industry or remained in public practice.

The choice confronting the young chartered accountant of remaining in practice or going into industry must largely be determined by personal preference, but it may not be inappropriate to consider some of the points he should keep in view in reaching his decision.

The accountant in practice is his own master. The services he renders to his clients are largely individual and his relationship with them is usually on a purely professional basis. In much of his work he is dealing with the same problems, but he will find variety in their application to different types of business. His work will take him into various parts of the country and he will meet all types of men. While his practice must be based on his integrity and professional skill, his success will largely be influenced by his personality. His satisfaction will be a knowledge of work well done and the confidence which his clients repose in his judgment and advice.

The accountant in industry, on the other hand, is one of a team. He must fit into the life of the company he joins, becoming one of the family, and his relationship with his colleagues will be on a more personal basis. His interests will be centred on one type of business but the problems confronting him can be endless in variety. He will find plenty of scope for his initiative in organising and possibly improving the accounting side of the business, and a wide field for research in accountancy and management technique. He must be a good administrator and be prepared to augment his professional knowledge by studying the technical and commercial side of the business. There is an almost infinite variety of positions he may hold and while his business career must be founded solidly on his integrity and professional skill, it will be largely influenced by his adaptability in adjusting himself to his new sphere of work.

It may well be that, with the development in the technique of management, the accountant in practice will be called on more and more to advise his clients on this subject, and the accountant who has acquired the practical experience from his work as an industrial accountant may in time return to public practice, perhaps as a specialist in this branch of the accountancy profession, but in any event with a wider and deeper knowledge of the problems he will meet in practice.

Different views are held as to the stage at which the change into industry is best made. It is held by some that the young accountant should enter industry as soon as possible after attaining his professional qualification and this view has been reinforced by the time which must elapse between starting an apprenticeship and finishing the period of National Service. Taking the longer view, however, it is felt that the young accountant has much to gain by remaining in the profession for one or two years after he has qualified. During this period he will extend his practical knowledge in his professional work and will also acquire that self-confidence which comes from undertaking more responsibility: at the same time he can pursue his studies in greater detail in the subjects which are specially appropriate for the accountant in industry.

Finally there is one aspect of the relationship between the accountant in industry and the professional body that must not be overlooked. No less important than the Institute's support of the accountant is the accountant's obligations to his profession and his support of the Institute. He must guard jealously his personal integrity, the good name of the Institute and the professional standards it enjoins. He must be unremitting in his search for truth and fearless in his presentation of facts. If the young industrial accountant can in the future conform to those same standards of training, proficiency and professional conduct that have been maintained over the past hundred years, an important and satisfying career is before him.

CHAPTER VII

THE APPRENTICE CHARTERED ACCOUNTANT

APPRENTICESHIP as a system of preparation for the professions can be traced back to the days of Ancient Egypt and Babylon and has been recognised legally in Scotland since mediæval times. The earliest references are to apprentices who were indentured to artisans and merchants, and the primary function was to provide practical training for young men by placing them in contact with, and under the direct instruction and influence of, fully qualified craftsmen or masters. In medicine and law the same method was followed for some centuries, and although in the former of these professions the system no longer applies, the law apprentice has still much in common with the apprentice in accountancy.

The chartered accountants of Scotland, as has been shown in previous chapters, have always attached the highest importance to apprenticeship as the method of entry into the qualified ranks of the profession; and many able and experienced members of the Institute to-day would testify with loyalty and enthusiasm that their success in life was founded on the example and teaching of their masters. The training so given deserves therefore some description and analysis in a separate chapter of this book.

Even before the formation of the three Scottish Societies, the apprenticeship system was not unknown to accountants. The advertisement of John Gibson and Robert Smellie quoted at page 12 suggests that in the eighteenth century accountancy was a recognised calling and one which required an apprenticeship for which parents would be prepared to pay a fee.

Shortly after its incorporation in 1854, The Society of Accountants in Edinburgh adopted Rules which set out a number of provisions relating to apprentices. Among other things, it was laid down that a five-year indenture should be served, and that candidates for indenture must be at least sixteen years of age, although there were concessions from the full period in certain circumstances. The apprentice fee payable to the master was fixed at one hundred guineas. Rules of a similar nature were adopted by The Institute of Accountants and Actuaries in Glasgow and The Society of Accountants in Aberdeen ; there were, however, certain variations. In Aberdeen the masters charged an apprentice a fee of forty guineas, while in Glasgow there was no regulation as to fees and it is understood that no fee was normally charged ; the duration of articles there was at first for a term of four years, and remained so until some time after the formation of the General Examining Board in 1892 when the period of five years' service was adopted. To-day the question whether any apprentice fee should be charged is a matter for arrangement between the parties to the indenture, and apprentices are remunerated on a scale recommended by the Council of the Institute.

A form of indenture closely approximating to that of to-day was in operation one hundred years ago and has its origins, indeed, in a period even earlier. Then, as now, an apprentice, if not of full age, required to have a cautioner, or guarantor ; and when the period of indenture was completed his master had to grant a discharge to the effect that the apprentice was fit to present himself for examination for admission.

By the indenture, as it runs to-day, the apprentice and his cautioner—who is usually his father—bind themselves that the apprentice will serve his master honestly, faithfully and diligently, that he will not reveal the secrets of his master's business and that he will behave decently, civilly and discreetly. The master, in his turn, covenants to teach and instruct his apprentice in all parts of the profession and employment of a chartered accountant and to conceal no part thereof from him, and to do his best to cause his apprentice to learn the same, so far as the apprentice is capable of learning. The execution of a deed of indenture is no mere formality, but a contractual agreement between master and apprentice, recognised by the Institute and

THE INSTITUTE'S HALL IN EDINBURGH

EXTERIOR

THE INSTITUTE'S HALL IN EDINBURGH

ENTRANCE

registered in its books, at which time a fee of ten guineas is chargeable.

Although the three Societies all recognised the need for recruiting their apprentices from among boys of a good educational standard, there was at first no preliminary examination relating to general education. Each Society in turn, however, instituted such an examination and for a long period this was compulsory to all candidates. At a later time the leaving certificate examination of the Scottish Education Department came to be recognised for this purpose, although the preliminary examination continued to be set by the General Examining Board. Later, certain other examinations were also recognised as qualifying and the preliminary examination ceased in 1911 to have a place among those set by the Board.

A candidate for indenture to-day must be at least seventeen years of age and must have the required preliminary qualification before his apprenticeship commences, or must obtain it during the first six months of his service. The preliminary qualifications now recognised by the Council of the Institute include certain passes in the Scottish Universities entrance examination, in the leaving certificate examination of the Scottish Education Department, or in the general certificate of education granted by certain other public examining bodies in the United Kingdom. The prescribed standard, which requires passes in English, Mathematics, a language other than English and at least one other subject, is designed to ensure that those who become apprentices are adequately prepared to meet the somewhat exacting requirements of the profession. A University degree approved by the Council is of course a qualification for indenture. Full details of what is required will be found in the General Summary of Rules for Admission of Members and Syllabus of Examinations, issued by the Institute.

Apart from the recognised scholastic qualifications, it is desirable that the general education of a prospective apprentice should have been on broad and sound lines. No exceptional ability in any one subject is required, but there are considerable advantages in having an aptitude for mathematics and an ability to use English with ease. There are some who consider that reasonable competence in Latin is also a good foundation for that clarity of thought and expression which is a very important attribute of a qualified accountant. And in a profession in which the use of the critical faculties is so very important, an apprentice will find that the possession and development of certain natural qualities will greatly benefit him during his training. These include imagination, perseverance, a reliable memory, wide powers of observation—even curiosity—and of deduction, quickness at grasping facts, willingness to accept responsibility, power of initiative, and general reliability—a formidable catalogue indeed.

More will be said later in this chapter on the subject of a University degree as a preliminary qualification for training, but it should be mentioned here that the Institute has approved what is sometimes termed a "sandwich course" whereby an apprentice who has served at least six months under indenture may attend a University, take a degree, and thereafter return to a professional office to complete his apprenticeship. In this case the period of apprenticeship is reduced to three years and six months, a reduction which is also granted to those who possess a recognised University degree before entering.

Having begun his period under indenture, an apprentice finds himself deeply involved in a course of training which is both practical and theoretical. The foundation is the practical training in the day-to-day business of an accountant which he receives in his office under the guidance and instruction of his master and senior members of the staff. The tutorial classes organised by the Institute and the compulsory classes at the Universities also have an important place; and success has never been achieved without a considerable amount of home study in the evenings and even at the week-ends.

The course of training nearly one hundred years ago was summarised in a lecture given in 1869 by Mr James McClelland, the first President of the Glasgow Institute. In this he says :—

"Let us begin with a youth fresh from the public schools and from college, entering the counting-house of parties in the usual employment of Chartered

Accountants. The youth, after writing out his own indenture, which is usually for a term of four years, enters upon the routine of all well-conducted offices. He soon finds that the education that he has obtained at school only gives him, in a more or less efficient form, according to the attention that he may have paid to his studies, the tools whereby he can be trained to the details of his profession. He soon masters many of these ; and at about the end of the second year of his work, he sees the necessity of becoming more intimately acquainted with the higher branches of arithmetic and algebra, with a more definite knowledge of the art of book-keeping, and learning for himself to note entries for books kept by double entry. His mind is led again to the knowledge of Commercial, Bankrupt and Civil Law ; and in order that he may be grounded in these branches of his profession, he finds it will be necessary for him to go back to school, and attend the prelections of the Professors of Commercial and Civil Law ; and in giving his mind to this branch of knowledge, again, that it will need at least two sessions at College, properly to follow out the study of these subjects."

The lecturer went on to point out the importance of studying the trade and commerce of the country, and particularly the trade with overseas. This was to lead to a study of foreign lands, and of the foreign exchanges. Bankruptcy, and the adjustment of all types of accounts ; the preparation of statements and reports ; the principles of life assurance and other branches of professional knowledge are all referred to as subjects for study before the student presented himself for examination for admission to the Institute.

From this it will be seen that although the emphasis on various subjects has changed in many ways and although new subjects for study have now been introduced, a sound and thorough training has always been considered essential.

The office training, as has been said, is considered fundamental, and here there have been many changes with the passing of the years. Another lecturer, sixty-five years ago, thus describes the office life of a junior apprentice at that period :—

" His work at first in most offices will be very simple. The use of the letter-copying press must be learned, and the indexing of the letter-book, the backing-up and orderly arrangement of letters and documents must be attended to, the correct keeping and accounting for stamps must be seen to, and then, after probably a year has been spent at such work, the youth may expect to get documents and statements and accounts to copy, from all which, if he has eyes open and mind intent on his work, he may learn lessons which will serve him to good purpose in after years."

This somewhat leisurely rate of progress would not, it is imagined, commend itself to the modern apprentice or to the office in which he is being trained.

There can be no doubt that in the early days of the profession, the office work was more simple—but it was also more thorough. As suitable text books and organised classes were fewer, the training given to apprentices then was probably of a more personal nature than is possible to-day. It seems likely that a much greater part of the apprentice's time was spent actually in his master's office (where working hours were long) and far less at audits in the offices of the firm's clients. The scope of knowledge required for the examinations was not so wide as to-day, but the standard demanded was, then as now, a high one, and there is no evidence that chartered accountants of the last century were any less proficient, in relation to the professional standards then required, than those of the present day.

We may now consider the training as it is carried out to-day in the offices of practising members. At the outset of the apprenticeship, it is made clear to the apprentices that a very high standard of work and conduct is expected of them. They must learn to stand on their own feet and take advantage of every chance given to them. The master impresses on them that they are joining a profession and that the ethics of the profession demand absolute confidentiality, integrity, honesty and loyalty in all matters with which they may have to deal. It is pointed out that they must work conscientiously and pay particular attention to accuracy and detail, that punctuality must be observed and dependability cultivated. They are encouraged to take a lively interest in all aspects of the profession and the work of the office ; their aim should be to widen their knowledge and so fit themselves for the responsibility which will eventually be entrusted to them. They should appreciate that throughout the period of their service they will receive the opportunities for gaining experience that they show themselves capable of absorbing.

It is natural that the breadth of experience which an apprentice receives during his service under indenture must depend to a large extent upon the size and character of his master's practice. A thorough grounding in book-keeping, some experience in auditing the books and accounts of private firms and of limited companies and a fair practice in the taxation matters of individuals and of companies may be expected in any professional office; in most offices there will in addition be opportunities for experience in some other branches of work such as company or other secretarial practice, trust auditing and accounting, cost accounting, investigations and reconstructions, and bankruptcy and liquidation work. For some apprentices it may be that the discipline of a larger office will prove beneficial; others may find that a smaller office may give them opportunities for more personal instruction and, possibly, greater variety of work.

Although the increasing use of office machinery—the typewriter, the adding machine, the postal franking machine and the duplicator—has done much to relieve present-day apprentices of irksome duties, there is still much to be said for arranging that the first few months of service under indenture should be spent in learning the elements of office procedure. Thus it is usually found that at the outset apprentices are introduced to the general office where they perform various duties under supervision. Some of these duties may appear elementary to the holder of a higher leaving certificate, but there are underlying principles to be learned and apprentices will find that if they perform with efficiency, patience and good humour their duties of filing, postage and banking—and even deliveries—they are acquiring knowledge, and in a few months' time when they become junior members of an audit team they will have gained sufficient confidence in themselves to perform useful and productive work on behalf of the firm. Here they will begin to find that everything they are called upon to do in the office is part of a larger, comprehensive programme each section of which is essential to the satisfactory completion of the work.

At an early stage it is desirable that apprentices should make a determined effort to understand the basic principles of book-keeping, since much of the work they will have to do will be related to it. While these principles have not changed for hundreds of years, methods have been adapted to changing conditions and the advent of mechanised accounting, whether partial or complete, has introduced a new element into the work. Nevertheless, the study of basic text books and the working of simple examples, coupled with the wide opportunities of seeing books of account which office training affords, should give the young apprentice a sound knowledge of this paramount subject, and even more so if he has the experience of keeping by himself a set of business books.

This practical training, combined with attendance at classes, brings the apprentice through the middle period of his indenture, and by the time the closing years approach he should be a useful member of the office team and should have accumulated a considerable fund of knowledge and experience of his future profession. He should by then have passed the intermediate examination and the first division of the final examination. He may on occasion overestimate the contribution that he is making to the office, but he will do well to realise that he has still much to learn and that his masters will give him the most suitable type of work at their disposal ; he must even be made to realise that there is something to be learned from the mere repetition of a process, such as auditing. Nevertheless, in this period, apprentices should be reaching a stage where they can carry work to its final stages with the minimum of supervision and should be preparing for the time when they will have to report, with their final notes, directly to a partner of their firm. The master for his part should see that the apprentice is informed of the final disposal of outstanding points, so that he may obtain a clear picture of what will be expected of him in the future. As the final examination approaches, an apprentice naturally finds that this is very much in the forefront of his mind and that attendance at classes is taking up a large amount of his time; he should not however on this account neglect in any way his office work, since this forms the practical basis to most of the subject-matter that he will find in the examination papers.

Of all the varied aspects of a chartered accountant's training, none is more important to the apprentices and to the future of the profession than office training sincerely and honestly carried out, both by masters and apprentices, in accordance with the terms of the indenture, the Rules of the Institute, and the accepted traditions of the profession.

The second main feature of professional training is class tuition. Apprentice chartered accountants have always found it helpful to have some tuition in the subjects included in the syllabus of the examinations and, with the considerable extension that has taken place in the diversity of an accountant's work, this need has grown steadily during the past century. Apart from the compulsory attendance at University classes which will be described later, the apprentice of one hundred years ago had to rely largely on the instruction he received from his masters, supplemented by study of the few text books then available. These text books—particularly in law, book-keeping, commercial arithmetic and algebra—were always adequate for the purpose, although modern techniques have of course improved the treatment of the various subjects and greatly increased the number of books published.

Private tuition for the examinations by accountants or schoolmasters was probably carried out from the earliest days, and before long it became apparent to the respective Societies that they had responsibilities in the matter of arranging instruction for their apprentices. At first this took the form of recognising and recommending classes of instruction which were set up by outside teachers, or courses of lectures which were arranged either by the Societies themselves or in conjunction with other bodies such as the Institute of Bankers. In Glasgow, the use of the Institute's Hall was granted for these classes and lectures from an early period. It was a time when the question of widening the general education of apprentices was much before the Councils both in Edinburgh and in Glasgow, and this lends interest to the fact that one course of lectures in Glasgow, held in 1877 in co-operation with the Institute of Bankers, covered the wide field of Natural History, Physiology and the Law of Bankruptcy. The lectures were delivered by three Professors in these subjects and are said to have been highly successful.

The first separate classes for apprentices were, it is thought, in the subject of Actuarial Science, but soon thereafter the need for classes in book-keeping and other professional subjects was recognised. This movement was accelerated by the formation in 1892 of the General Examining Board for the Chartered Accountants of Scotland, and before the end of the century classes, both on intermediate and final standards, were well organised in Edinburgh, Glasgow and Aberdeen.

As the numbers coming forward increased and the range of the examinations widened, so the classes grew and multiplied. The appointment in all centres of Directors of Studies by the respective Societies and the formation of Tutorial Classes Committees led to better organisation and enabled apprentices to plan their courses of study to greater advantage. Later, the large numbers of apprentices returning from the First World War and the equally large number of new entrants to the profession in the same period gave rise to even greater needs; class-room accommodation at the premises of the Societies in Edinburgh and Glasgow has been extended on several occasions to meet these growing requirements.

The system of classes to-day in Edinburgh, Glasgow and London is indeed comprehensive. In Aberdeen and in Dundee, the range of classes is also wider than before and, though in other centres it is not possible to arrange classes of instruction, improved communications probably permit many apprentices from a wider radius to take some advantage at least of these facilities. The classes held are constantly under review so that their scope keeps pace with the varying requirements of the examinations and the profession.

The classes organised to-day by the Institute are primarily intended as a preparation for the examinations. They are conducted mainly by members in practice who give their services on a part-time basis. The whole system is co-ordinated at the various centres by the Directors of Studies who also hold individual interviews with apprentices and guide them on their courses of study. The normal method in the classes is to issue notes and give oral and blackboard instruction in the mathematical subjects, in certain parts of law, and in the theory and practice of accounting. Practical examples are worked out in class and test questions are also issued to students as homework, so that apprentices receive ample opportunity of preparing written answers. Although attendance at tutorial classes is not compulsory, it is strongly recommended, and regularity of attendance and conscientious preparation of homework are also stressed as desirable. Students are in addition encouraged to make use of the very comprehensive facilities offered by the Institute's libraries where large numbers of standard text books and accountancy publications are held. It can certainly be said in Scotland that no apprentice of the Institute need suffer from a lack of the text books he requires.

It is understood that the Scottish Institute is the only body of professional accountants in the United Kingdom which provides tutorial classes in connection with its examinations. The Institute and the profession in general owe much to the inauguration of these classes and to the men who, over the years, have organised and conducted them. As a tribute to their efforts it is interesting to record that for the Spring Session 1954 the number of enrolments for the classes at the various centres was 1,918.

The connection between the Scottish Universities and the accountancy profession is an old one, dating back to the time before the Charters. Attendance at various law classes in Edinburgh, Glasgow and Aberdeen was the first form of instruction outside the office prescribed for apprentices, and although the classes to be attended have varied from time to time at each centre, instruction in law at the Universities has always been a compulsory requirement.

The emphasis has naturally been on mercantile law with which professional work is so closely connected, but at various times apprentices have attended, or have been encouraged to attend, classes in Scots Law, Civil Law and Conveyancing. The mercantile law itself has of course increased greatly in volume during the last hundred years and there are now many Acts of Parliament which an apprentice must master. Hence of later years the emphasis has been more and more concentrated on this branch of the law, although a knowledge of general principles in other branches is still, as always, beneficial, particularly to an accountant in public practice.

Another subject which early found a place in the syllabus was Political Economy and in this the facilities at the Universities have always been used in one form or another. In Edinburgh full attendance at the Political Economy class at the University is now compulsory ; in other centres, shortened courses organised by the Universities by arrangement with the Institute are considered sufficient. The Institute does not now examine in Political Economy but a pass at the appropriate University examination is essential.

More recently, Accountancy has become a University subject involving compulsory attendance on the part of apprentices. The founding of the Chairs of Accountancy at Edinburgh and Glasgow has been described in Chapter IV, and the classes there are now a recognised and important feature of the course of study. In Aberdeen there are facilities for apprentices to attend a University class in Accounting ; in Dundee a compulsory class in Advanced Accounting is organised by the Institute and in London classes of a standard comparable to the Scottish Universities are organised by arrangement with the London Local Committee of the Institute with the approval of the Council.

An apprentice chartered accountant attending a University class is also a matriculated student of the University with all the rights and privileges that matriculation confers. It cannot be said that in general apprentices, with their long hours of office work and private study, are able to make much use of these privileges ; but there are exceptions, and apprentices do in some cases take their part, with much advantage to themselves, in various aspects of University life.

A much closer connection exists where an apprentice already possesses a University degree or is studying concurrently for one. The place of the accountant who also possesses a University qualification has always been an honoured one, and many outstanding members of the three former Societies and of the Institute have been University graduates. It has often been contended that accountancy, despite an insistence on a broad and liberal education, may become a somewhat narrow career. This need not necessarily be so ; but there is no doubt that a University graduate, who has taken a degree before commencing his course in accountancy, has acquired by extensive reading a cultural background and a trained mind which will be of great value in his career. The enjoyment of facilities for sport and mixing with others and the wise use of leisure during his University days will have added something to his character which other apprentices have not necessarily acquired. It must be recognised, however, that for the great majority of apprentices a full University career is not possible ; but it should also be recognised that many of those so qualified have in fact made a distinctive contribution to the profession. The inauguration of the "sandwich course" referred to earlier in this chapter and now recognised and approved by the Institute and the University authorities will undoubtedly give greater opportunities for a double qualification.

All office experience and attendance at classes leads up to the final examination on which admission to the Institute, or to the earlier Societies, has always depended. That the examinations have, over the years, become more testing cannot be denied ; but this has merely been in accordance with the greater demands made by all professions and the examinations of the Institute are not, and never have been, competitive.

There was at first only a final examination, as it would now be termed, and this was taken at the end of the period of apprenticeship. It may be interesting to quote in full the earliest Rules relating to the matter.

Rule 39 of the Edinburgh Society stated :—

"Candidates for admission shall undergo examination by the Examinators at such time and place as they may appoint. The Examinators shall examine Candidates for admission in such form and to such extent as they may consider necessary upon subjects usually occurring in the practice of the profession, such as algebra, including the use of logarithms—annuities—life assurances—liferents—reversions—book-keeping—framing of states under sequestrations, trusts, factories, executries—the Law of Scotland, especially that relating to Bankruptcy, private trust and arbitration, rights and preferences of creditors in rankings."

Rule 41 adopted by the Glasgow Institute almost immediately after its incorporation was in the following terms :—

"That in future it shall be required that applicants for admission shall undergo an examination, and that the examination shall imply a knowledge on the part of the applicant of the elementary principles of the Bankruptcy Law, of Book-keeping and Accounts, of the practical working of Bankruptcy, Trust Estates, Voluntary and Judicial Factories and of the rudimentary principles of Arithmetic and Algebra."

It is not necessary here to trace the various changes introduced into their respective examinations by the three Societies, but it is interesting to record that in the earliest days failures in the final examinations were almost unknown. Despite this happy state of affairs, it may well be that the examination then was just as much of an ordeal to the candidates as it now is. With the smaller numbers in the profession in those days, however, a candidate's abilities were probably fairly well known personally to some at least of the committee of examiners when he appeared before them.

At the time of the formation of the General Examining Board in 1892 the examination papers were as follows :—

Preliminary Examination

This examination consisted of five papers of one hour's duration as follows :—

Writing to dictation, English Grammar and Composition.
Arithmetic (Elementary).

These subjects were compulsory and candidates had to elect to be examined further on three of the following subjects :—

British History.
Geography of the World, with special reference to the Geography of Great Britain, her Colonies and the Continent of Europe.
Geometry—Euclid Book I.
Shorthand—Dictation and Transcription.
Latin, including grammar and short translations.
French or German, including grammar and short translations.

Intermediate Examination

Mathematics—Advanced Arithmetic and Algebra.
Professional Knowledge—Book-keeping, Framing Accounts and Correspondence.

Final Examination

Law of Scotland relating to Bankruptcies, Judicial Factories, Companies, Partnerships, etc.
Actuarial Science.
Political Economy.
General Business of an Accountant, comprising :—

(*a*) Theory and practice of Book-keeping ;
(*b*) Preparation of Balance Sheets and Profit and Loss Accounts ;
(*c*) Audit of Accounts ;
(*d*) Trust Accounts ;
(*e*) Schemes of Division ;
(*f*) Bankruptcies and Liquidations ;
(*g*) References, Remits and Proofs.

It may be interesting to mention that the results of the December 1893 examinations were as follows :—

	Entrants	*Passed*	*Failed*
Preliminary . . .	50	39	11
Intermediate . .	33	25	8
Final . . .	13	9	4
	96	73	23

Similar statistics relating to the results in later years will be found in Appendix VIII.

In 1906 the General Examining Board issued a new syllabus to come into operation in December of that year. In the intermediate examination the papers then included annuities certain and précis writing along with correspondence. The most interesting changes, however, occurred in the final examination, where the principles of cost accounts and income tax were included for the first time.

In 1911 the final papers were again re-arranged, without this time introducing anything further of vital importance, and at the same time it was decided to withdraw the preliminary examination, although apprentices still required to qualify for entry into the profession by obtaining one of the qualifications already mentioned which had formerly entitled them to exemption from this examination.

In 1922 the book-keeping paper of the intermediate examination was considerably extended to include departmental and branch accounts and consignment and joint adventure accounts, which had hitherto formed part of the final examination. Précis writing was excluded from the intermediate examination. At this time two of the papers of the final examination appear to have been complementary, one of them dealing with the theory and practice of book-keeping and the other with the preparation of accounting statements and the higher elements of accountancy.

In 1931 the Examining Board divided the intermediate examination into two divisions which had to be taken separately, and in 1933 it decided that the final examination should similarly be taken in two divisions. Until this latter date, candidates could elect to take either the entire final examination at one diet or one division at a time, although for some years the latter had been the almost universal practice.

At the present time the examinations consist of the following:—

INTERMEDIATE

Division I

(1) Arithmetic and Algebra.
(2) Elementary Finance and Statistics.

Division II

(3) Theory and practice of Book-keeping, including the preparation of Balance Sheets, Manufacturing Trading and Profit and Loss Accounts, Departmental and Branch Accounts, Consignment and Joint Adventure Accounts.
(4) Auditing of Commercial Accounts, elementary Income Tax, Interest States, office routine, the meaning and use of business terms, correspondence, agenda and minutes of meetings, etc.

FINAL

Division I

(1) Law of Scotland concerning Contract, Bills of Exchange, Sale of Goods, general principles of insurance, insolvency, bankruptcy, trust deeds for creditors and sequestration.
(2) Law of Scotland relating to Joint Stock Companies, Partnership, Trusts and Judicial Factories including Fee and Liferent and Apportionment, Testate and Intestate Succession and Legal Rights.
(3) Trust and Executry Accounts, Schemes of Division under Trusts and in Intestacy including in both cases claims for Legal Rights, Fee and Liferent, Apportionments.

Division II

(4) Advanced Book-keeping, the preparation of Accounts including Group Accounts.
(5) Cost Accounts, Business Statistics and Budgetary Control.
(6) Income Tax, Surtax and Profits Tax.
(7) The investigation of Accounts and preparation of Reports thereon, States of Affairs in Insolvencies, Bankruptcies and Liquidations including Schemes of Ranking and Division, the Duties of Arbiters and Referees and the preparation of Statements in connection with Arbitrations, Remits and Proofs, General Financial Knowledge including the practice and terminology of Banking, the Stock Exchange and the National Budget.
(8) Auditing of all classes of Accounts.

A period of three and a half hours is allowed for papers (3) and (4) of the intermediate examination and papers (3) to (8) of the final examination: for the other papers a period of three hours is the permitted time.

In connection with the examinations, certain prize funds formerly held by the Glasgow Institute for the benefit of candidates there are now vested in the Scottish Institute and are awarded if papers of sufficient merit are submitted and subject to certain other qualifications. The prizes are as follows :—

The John Mann Prize awarded annually to the candidate who passes the second division of the final examination with the highest percentage of marks.

The Albert J. Watson Prize awarded at each examination diet to the candidate who achieves the highest percentage of marks in the first division of the final examination.

The Sir William McLintock Prize awarded to the two candidates who obtain the highest percentage of marks at each diet of the second division of the intermediate examination.

The Guthrie Prize awarded to the best woman candidate to qualify in the final examination each year.

Diets of Examination are held in May and December of each year in Edinburgh, Glasgow, Aberdeen, Dundee and London and are administered by the Examining Board, which is composed almost entirely of practising members of the Institute who set and mark the papers. It is appropriate that this should continue so, as it ensures that in setting questions emphasis is laid on practical experience.

Much has been heard about the difficulties experienced by some students in passing the Institute's examinations.. It is not the general opinion of qualified and experienced members of the profession that the examinations are too difficult. No young man—or woman—of character and reasonable ability, who goes through the system of training conscientiously and who applies himself and works hard, need have any fears about his prospects of qualifying. Certainly the examination syllabus has become wider with the years, and more emphasis is placed on subjects such as costing and taxation than was the case some years ago, but it must also be said that the examiners have always set out to test a candidate's knowledge of a wide range of subjects at a reasonable level.

While stress is placed on the value of a sound practical training in a professional office, students will do well to realise that they have also to acquire a large amount of theoretical knowledge. Although during apprenticeship most of the study has perforce to be done in the evenings or at week-ends, the Institute recommends the granting of leave from office work

THE INSTITUTE'S HALL IN EDINBURGH

PART OF THE LIBRARY

THE INSTITUTE'S HALL IN EDINBURGH

THE MAIN STAIRCASE

for short periods immediately before the examinations in order that candidates may then be relieved of the strain of attempting to study after a full day's office work. This also is intended to give candidates more time for out-door exercise, for it is essential that they should keep fit.

In the foregoing paragraphs, a description has been given of the main features of training and examination as they exist at the present time and, for historical interest, some description of earlier methods has also been given. It would not be claimed that the present arrangements are perfect and it cannot be denied that some people have alternative suggestions to make for entry into the qualified ranks of the profession; of these suggestions one is a long period of academic study, coupled with a series of attachments from time to time in industrial establishments and professional offices. In order to ensure that all these questions are properly reviewed, the Council of the Institute in 1953 appointed a Committee on the Training and Examination of Apprentices. The membership was carefully selected to ensure that all interests were represented and the terms of reference are wide. The Committee began its proceedings by issuing a questionnaire to which replies have been submitted by many individuals and groups, and these replies are now under consideration. When in due course this Committee submits its Report, it can safely be assumed that any changes that may be recommended will be the result of careful deliberation and will receive very serious consideration from the Council of the Institute and from the body of members.

No account of the apprenticeship system in the profession in Scotland would be complete without some notes on the Chartered Accountants Students' Societies, because these have for many years been an important feature in Edinburgh, Glasgow and Aberdeen. Membership of the Societies is open to qualified chartered accountants as well as to apprentices, and it is true that the former have always taken the leading part in the management of the Societies. The benefits of membership are, however, of the greatest importance to apprentices and a number of the activities are exclusively for them.

The Chartered Accountants Students' Society of Edinburgh was formed in 1886 and its existence has continued until the present time. In Glasgow, in 1887, a Debating Society for younger qualified members and apprentices was formed with the approval and support of the Institute. After some years this Society disappeared but was succeeded in 1899 by The Glasgow Chartered Accountants Students' Society which is still in existence. In Aberdeen a Students' Society was established prior to 1904.

The mainstay of the syllabus in each Society has always been the lecture. Beginning at a time when class instruction was not so highly organised as it is now, these lectures have covered a wide field. Some distinguished lecturers, including many from the Scottish Bar and a large number of eminent accountants from England, as well as members of the profession in Scotland, have contributed to the series. Many of these lectures have been published. There are twenty-five volumes of Transactions of the Edinburgh Society, running from 1887, while the Glasgow Society has twelve volumes running from 1902. In 1921, the two Societies agreed to publish their Transactions jointly, and to date twenty-five volumes in this series have appeared. These books contain a wealth of information, much of which is still of value—and it is quite surprising how often some problem encountered in practice can be solved by consulting an old volume of the Students' Societies' Transactions.

The Societies have of course had other activities. There have been debates and joint meetings, in Edinburgh with the Scots Law Society and in Glasgow with the Glasgow Juridical Society. In 1909 the first joint discussion between the Edinburgh and Glasgow Societies took place. Discussions on the intermediate and final examinations were a regular feature of the syllabus.

In 1920 the Glasgow Students' Society began to set test examinations. These, although absolutely independent, were based on the same syllabus as the professional examinations set by the General Examining Board and it was soon found that they gave valuable experience to those apprentices who chose to enter for them. In the following year the Students' Societies of Glasgow and Edinburgh set joint test examinations and since then these have continued in conjunction with the Aberdeen Students' Society; special arrangements are also made for students who wish to sit the examinations in Dundee. The test examinations are now among the most important activities of the three Students' Societies.

A more recent activity has been the inauguration of a series of conducted visits to public offices and large factories in Edinburgh and Glasgow. This innovation has proved popular with apprentices and may make a useful contribution to the syllabus of the future.

Social functions have always been an important feature of the Students' Societies and have been very valuable in bringing members together in an atmosphere far removed from the office or the class-room. As far back as 1897, smoking concerts were held by the Edinburgh Students' Society and in 1921 its first annual dance was held: the Chartered Accountants Students' Society ball is now an important annual social occasion in Edinburgh. In Glasgow, dinners were the main form of social activity for many years and an outstandingly successful series of banquets was held in the years preceding the First World War; the dinners were afterwards resumed and, generally, took place every second year. A notable dinner was held in 1949 to mark the occasion of the fiftieth anniversary of the Society. Dances have, more recently, been organised in Glasgow also and the annual dance of the Students' Society is now, as in Edinburgh, a well established event.

Organised sporting activities began in Edinburgh in 1924 when an inter-office golf competition was instituted, and this was followed in 1931 by an inter-office tennis tournament. In recent years an annual rugby football match has been played between Edinburgh and Glasgow. In Glasgow inter-office football matches have been played for some years. Similar events, including a lawn tennis tournament in Aberdeen, have from time to time been held in other centres.

The objects of Students' Societies are primarily to benefit apprentices by providing for them a common meeting place where they will have wider opportunities for educational training and for discussing their problems with other members. It is beyond question that the profession as a whole benefits from their activities. The Institute recognises the value of the work the Students' Societies do and contributes regularly to their funds. A large number of chartered accountants continue membership of the Students' Societies and are willing and anxious to help in their activities.

Students' Societies enable their members to obtain an insight into professional life and give them the opportunity of acquiring knowledge of many important matters which cannot be dealt with in the office or the class-room. They enable younger members to assimilate the atmosphere of the profession and give admirable opportunities for public speaking and for learning something of the procedure and conduct of business meetings. There must be many chartered accountants to-day who have the Students' Societies to thank for giving them confidence and courage in their first public appearances. Meetings of the Societies, for which a syllabus is prepared and issued each autumn, are held between October and March.

The apprentice chartered accountant is fortunate in having his Students' Society. The atmosphere among members of all the Societies is and has always been extremely cordial. It is perhaps a pity that the very size of the Societies in Edinburgh and Glasgow makes it impossible for all to take a positive and active part in the deliberations, but despite this there is much to be gained from membership and attendance at all the meetings. The Students' Societies help to promote a mutual association and exchange of ideas among members which goes far beyond formal education but is yet in close accord with the ideas and objects of the founders of the profession a century ago.

THE INSTITUTE'S HALL IN EDINBURGH

The Council Room

THE GLASGOW INSTITUTE'S FORMER HALL IN WEST NILE STREET

This chapter has traced the apprenticeship and training system to the point where the next step is admission to membership of the Institute. But a word should be said about the apprentice himself, before he is admitted—the product that it has taken five years to finish.

Individually, no doubt, apprentices, who may hail from anywhere between the County of Caithness and the City of London—or even farther afield—are a diverse collection of young men, and there is no standard type. The somewhat mythical figure of the Scottish chartered accountant, with a considerable fund of logic and of moral rectitude, who is said to crop up all over the world, somewhat as does the Scottish engineer, is really an abstraction of qualities which the hard training of the profession inculcates. The apprentice, in his younger days, has as yet no such shape ; his home circumstances and educational background vary within wide limits, and his office training, which may take place in industrial city or country town, must also manifest wide variations.

Yet this chapter will have gone astray if it has not indicated, or suggested, some of the common qualities and qualifications that may be looked for in every apprentice at the end of his period of training. He will certainly have failed —even though he may have passed every examination and obtained every class ticket—if he has not learned to look beyond the examinations and to prepare himself for a useful working life, either in public practice or in the service of industry. He should have assimilated considerable knowledge, not only of examination subjects, but of the profession, its work, procedures, traditions and prestige. He ought to have an ethical attitude, and an objective approach, to every problem presented to him, and where he does not carry the required knowledge in his head, he should certainly know where to obtain it. Even when he has passed the final examination—and after this event has been duly celebrated—he should realise that he has still much to learn about the conduct of business ; but at the same time he should have confidence in his own ability for further learning.

We do not have many pictures of apprentices of one hundred years ago, although some old photographs of office groups give interesting suggestions. Then a high linen collar and clothing of dark hue were obviously essential; an incipient moustache may have been an advantage. To-day a much more informal dress is probably tolerated in most offices. Much has been said about the fine penmanship of apprentices in the early era, and some of it may possibly be true. Many members to-day can recall how the fountain pen was regarded in most offices as an abomination, and one may be permitted to wonder what some of the seniors of the profession would say about the ball-pointed pens whose use is so widespread to-day. One hears also of amazing prowess, long years ago, at adding immense columns of figures, but the modern apprentice would scorn such waste of time if an adding machine were available even two miles away. A taste for coffee is said to be common to all apprentices; one does not know whether the liquids of a century ago were so innocuous or so time-consuming; probably they were.

It should be said that through the years apprentices have borne their fair share, as citizens, of National Service. Some went overseas in the South African War, and great numbers volunteered for service in the First World War, notably in such units as The Royal Scots and The Glasgow Chamber of Commerce Battalion, as the 17th Battalion of the Highland Light Infantry was known. Many became commissioned officers and many made the supreme sacrifice. In the Second World War the system of calling up was somewhat more scientific, and after the first batch of members of the Territorial Army and Naval and Air Force Reserves—of whom there were many—had gone away, there was at first a pause. From thence onwards, apprentices who had already had a year or two of office life in the difficult conditions of war time were gradually called up and in many cases the finish of the war found them thousands of miles away from home; from this war also a considerable number did not return. The period of readjustment that followed has not been without its difficulties, but nothing should be allowed to dim the recollection of the valuable service that these young men gave to their country in time of need. Since the introduction of National Service in peace time the young accountant is liable at some part of his career to perform two years of full-time military training.

We reach the stage, therefore, when the candidate's application for admission, sponsored by two members, has been approved by the Council, and the entry fee of forty guineas has been paid. The young member is admitted by the Institute in General Meeting and he has received his certificate of admission, signed by the President. His career lies now before him: it may be in practice in this country or overseas; in industry or commerce; in Government service, or in one of the nationalised industries. In whichever of these it may be, he will find that among his most valuable assets is the qualification and membership of his Institute, and he cannot do better than to take to heart the words spoken by one of the founders of the profession in a lecture delivered many years ago to which reference has already been made:—

"The work in which the young Chartered Accountant will now be engaged will be small at the beginning. He cannot look for his friends or the public appreciating, in the early days of his career, either the talents he may naturally possess, or the labour he has passed through in qualifying himself for the profession. He may thus, like many men in other walks of life, have to wait upon the tide as it flows; but if he is true to himself, it will doubtless rise, with full and profitable employment in his calling. He has therefore only to persevere—to give undeviating attention even to the smallest matter of business offered to him—to execute, with the fidelity and the ability he must have acquired through the training imparted to him, any trust or business in which he may be employed. Let him keep honest, truthful and accurate accounts, wherever money matters are concerned. Let him seek out, in opinions which he may be required to give—in accounts he has to frame—and in reports he has to prepare, the strict principles of integrity and justice, neither leaning to one side nor the other; but looking on himself as an arbiter to do Justice to all. He may come, by pursuing such a course, to find himself inimical sometimes to the views, and sometimes to the interest, of parties concerned; but let him not swerve from his duty. He will thus acquire the confidence of the public, and the reputation of an independent and trustworthy member of his profession."

CHAPTER VIII

THE INSTITUTE'S HALLS AND LIBRARIES

PROMINENT among the objects that the founders of the Chartered Societies had in view were the acquisition of halls, or premises, and the building up of adequate libraries of professional books. The purchase or building of a hall would, it was thought, give stability to the profession; and the institution of a good library was an obvious convenience to members at a time when books were relatively less plentiful and more expensive than they subsequently became. Again, the profession was following the practice of other professions at that time: the various societies or faculties of writers, procurators, surgeons, physicians and others had halls and libraries.

Despite the importance of these objects, however, there were practical considerations which for a time prevented their full achievement. The most compelling of these was perhaps the question of ways and means; the Societies in their early days did not have the funds available. In Edinburgh the acquisition of premises did not take place until after the establishment of the Endowment and Annuity Fund, which was given priority and which absorbed a substantial part of the accumulated funds of the Society. In Glasgow, a hall was purchased at an earlier date, but the transaction was financed for a time by borrowed money. In both cities it was only after premises had been purchased and a permanent home for the possessions of the Societies had so been secured that the libraries began to grow in size and importance. In Aberdeen no premises were acquired, but a library was established at an early date and soon proved its usefulness to the members there.

In this chapter the history of the premises owned at first by the Societies and now by the Institute will be related and an account will be given of the establishment and growth of the libraries.

Among the powers taken by the Edinburgh Society in the Bye-Laws, Rules and Regulations adopted in 1855 after the grant of the Charter was a power to invest the funds in the purchase of heritable property; and it is clear from various minutes of the early period that there was a desire among the members that the Society should have a permanent home. Meetings of the Society were at first held in various halls and rooms, and the President and Council met in the office of the Secretary or other offices. Proposals were from time to time made for acquiring premises in which to hold meetings and to house the library, but although various projects were examined by committees appointed for the purpose, the views of the Society were not unanimous as to the places recommended or, indeed, as to the immediate necessity for taking the step.

At the Annual Meeting in 1890, the question was again raised, and the matter was left in the hands of the President and Council for further action. By the time of the meeting in 1891 such action had been taken and the President was able to report that it was proposed to purchase premises at No. 27 Queen Street, and a motion that this purchase be approved was unanimously carried. The first meeting of the Society within its new Hall was held on February 3, 1892, and thenceforward all its meetings were held there. On the formation of The Institute of Chartered Accountants of Scotland in 1951 these premises became part of the headquarters of the Institute.

The premises, No. 27 Queen Street, later added to by the purchase of Nos. 26, 28 and 29, form part of the original frontage of the street as laid out in 1789. The land on which the property is built belonged at one time to the Trustees of George Heriot, a wealthy citizen of Edinburgh and the King's goldsmith. He followed King James VI to England in 1603, and was so successful that when he died in 1624 he was able, like George Watson, who has been mentioned in Chapter I, to leave a large fortune for the endowment of a school for boys, still one of the best known in Edinburgh and one at which many future chartered accountants were to have their early education. Before the construction of the New Town of Edinburgh in the latter part of the eighteenth century, the land—which then bore the perhaps rather unprophetic name of Barefoots Park—is understood to have been feued by the Heriot Trustees to the Provost and Magistrates. At this time the north side of the ridge on which the New Town is built was farm and woodland, sloping gently down towards the Firth of Forth and with a magnificent view of the mountains to the north.

The Town in its turn feued various sites in Queen Street to those who built the original houses. The exterior aspect of the whole street, with its tall, grey stone-built houses and the pleasure gardens across the way in front, has not changed very much in the last 150 years; and the Edinburgh Society on making its purchases was wise not to alter the simple yet dignified exterior of the properties, although behind the façade much of the interior has been completely reconstructed. The first owners were professional people—advocates, writers to the Signet and doctors, at that period generally regarded as the wealthier classes. No. 27 was purchased from the family of Lieutenant-General Alexander Graham Stirling, who was a notable soldier of his day and who occupied the house for many years.

On entering into possession, the Edinburgh Society arranged for various alterations to be made under the supervision of Mr Thomas Leadbetter, Architect, to equip the premises for their new purposes. The accounts for the year 1891 show that the price of the house and the cost of alterations, fittings and furniture was £5,511. A hall was provided, and also a library, reading room, writing room, smoking room and caretaker's house. The first rules of the hall show that the premises were open every week day from 9 A.M. to 10 P.M.; tea and coffee were available; and it was laid down that no dogs were to be admitted. It was soon found by members and their apprentices that the new rooms served many useful purposes and they began to play an important part in the various activities of the Society.

Before very long examinations began to be held there; all Edinburgh members are familiar with the aspect of the main hall in which they were admitted to the Society, and one member has recorded how many of his recollections centre there, because within its walls he attended his first class, sat all his examinations (glancing resentfully at the old clock!), was admitted a member of the Society, and gave his first lecture to students; here also he spent happy hours as chairman or lecturer at numerous Students' Society meetings. There must be many others with similar recollections.

By 1908 No. 27 Queen Street was wholly occupied by the Edinburgh Society. The need for further expansion was foreseen and in the same year the opportunity was taken of purchasing No. 26 Queen Street for £4,030. It is recorded that £320 was spent on alterations to No. 26 at about that time and that it was at first let to various tenants. In 1923, however, it was decided to make alterations so as to convert Nos. 26 and 27 into a single property for the use of the Society. This work was undertaken under the supervision of Messrs Leadbetter, Fairley & Reid, Architects, and was completed in 1925 at a cost of £4,650.

The next expansion of the Society's premises occurred in 1948, when Nos. 28 and 29 came into the market and were purchased for £16,000. Until the amalgamation of the three Scottish Chartered Societies in 1951 these two houses continued to be occupied by tenants, but in 1952 work was started under the supervision of Messrs J. D. Cairns & Ford, Architects, on converting No. 28 for use as the main offices of the Institute. The alterations then made included the provision of a new class room and an additional public room for the use of members. The major part of the work was completed by the end of 1952, the total cost being £7,250. Internal connections now exist between Nos. 26, 27 and 28, and the three buildings are now virtually a single unit with a single main entrance. No. 29 remains let to tenants, but could one day be used for further expansion by the Institute if this were to prove necessary.

On passing through the main doorway of No. 27, the panelled entrance hall is seen, and on each wall there are the War Memorials to members who gave their lives in the two World Wars. To the right of the entrance hall are the offices of the Institute; to the left are the library and reading rooms. The staircase, at the back of the entrance hall, is of graceful proportions, and leads up to the main hall and thence to the Council room.

The main hall, on the first floor, is a handsome room which seats about 150 persons. On the walls there hang the portraits and photographs of past Presidents of the Edinburgh Society and there may also be observed a fine marble bust of Charles Selkrig, one of the most distinguished accountants of his day, regarding whom some details are given in Chapter I. On this floor also is the Council room, which faces Queen Street. It is a dignified room, well-suited for its purpose, and its walls are embellished by a series of handsome engravings which were recently presented to the Institute by Mrs Greenhill, widow of Mr William Greenhill who was President of the Edinburgh Society from 1928 to 1931. Other engravings from the same collection are hung on the walls of the main staircase and in other rooms in the building. The upper floors also contain various committee rooms and class rooms, well equipped for their purposes.

It seems certain that for many years these premises, with their old associations and traditions, will meet the needs of the Institute in Edinburgh in their various requirements of meeting places, class and examination rooms, library and administrative offices. Their situation happily combines the advantages of a central business position in a dignified street with a fresh, open frontage which seems unlikely to be disturbed.

The first rules of the Glasgow Institute, adopted on its formation in 1853, make it clear that the acquisition of a

THE INSTITUTE'S HALL IN GLASGOW
Entrance Hall and Main Staircase

THE INSTITUTE'S HALL IN GLASGOW

St Vincent Street Frontage

suitable hall was then in contemplation. Rule 12 begins as follows :—

"The funds thus obtained (*i.e.*, from entry monies and annual contributions) shall be applied by the Council in defraying the current expenses of the Institute and in leasing and furnishing, or when attainable purchasing and furnishing premises for the use of the Institute, and for such other purposes as shall be recommended and approved by a quarterly or special meeting of the Institute . . ."

The headquarters of the Institute, at which all its meetings were held, were at first located in the rooms of the Stock Exchange in the National Bank Buildings, Queen Street, demolished many years ago. The minutes record that by courtesy of the Committee of the Stock Exchange this accommodation was offered to the Institute at a rental for each meeting of 10s. for the large hall and 5s. for the small room, or alternatively at an annual rental of £10 for all the rooms, provided that the hours of meeting of the Stock Exchange were not interfered with. The latter alternative was, in the words of the minute, "deemed the best and most dignified for the Institute" and was accepted.

Since a large number of the members of the Institute were, as has already been related, members of the Stock Exchange also, this arrangement appears to have worked satisfactorily, and it lasted for nearly twenty years. By that time, it was becoming apparent that if the Institute was to make progress separate premises for meetings and for the accommodation of an expanding library were desirable ; at the Annual Meeting in 1870 the Council was instructed by the members to take action in this matter and several projects were investigated by a committee, at first without success.

Early in 1873, however, it was learned that a two-storey building, No. 106 West Nile Street, was for sale. This building which still stands opposite the junction of West Nile Street with West Regent Street, was formerly occupied by an establishment known as the Victoria Baths under the charge of a Mr T. F. Tracey, Surgeon Dentist and Chiropodist. The premises adjoining were occupied by Henglers Cirque, or Circus, a well-known place of entertainment in Glasgow for many years. It appeared to the Council that this building was suitable in every way for the purposes of the Institute, and at a special meeting held on February 10, 1873, it was decided to purchase the premises for a sum of £5,500, and that the portion of the purchase price in excess of the funds of the Institute should be met by borrowing on the security of a heritable bond on the premises.

The alterations necessary to convert the buildings for their new use were soon put in hand, and the minutes show that the members of the Council took an active interest in the matter. Under the direction of Mr John Burnet, Architect, the ground floor and out-buildings were divided and let to two tenants. The upper floor was arranged to provide a large hall, which also became the library, and a small room in which the Council met. The total cost, including the alterations, was £7,000 and as the property contained 443 square yards this worked out at £15, 16s. per yard—a figure which it may be interesting to compare with present-day standards. Here the 20th Annual General Meeting of the Institute was held on January 27, 1874, and also a Celebration Dinner on March 9 under the presidency of Mr William Anderson.

These buildings were to be the home of the Glasgow Institute for the next 25 years. There, there were held all meetings of members, the examinations and, in course of time, lectures and classes. The library flourished and grew, and increasing use of it was made by the members. In the newspapers of the period the announcement "Creditors to meet in The Accountants' Hall" became increasingly frequent.

A time arrived however when the Hall in West Nile Street became insufficient for the growing needs of the Institute. Again, it is interesting to note that the initiative for a removal came from the body of members who apparently were not satisfied that the necessary diligence in this matter was being exercised by the Council. The subject had first been raised at the Annual Meeting in 1892, and in April 1894 there was sent to the Council a petition signed by 88 members, out of a membership of about 200, urging the sale of the property and the acquisition of premises more worthy of the standing of the Institute and more suitable for the requirements and accommodation of the members and students. It was generally agreed however that the old hall must be sold before a new one was purchased; and it appears that this was not an easy task because it was not until January 26, 1898, that the property was ultimately disposed of at a price of £7,500.

One of the last acts of the Council in connection with the old premises was to grant permission to the Glasgow Corporation Tramways Committee to affix to the wall of the building a bracket in connection with the wiring for the new electric tramcars. This recalls that Mr James Dalrymple, then Accountant to the Tramways Department and later for many years the Tramways Manager, was an active member of the Institute; he achieved in his day a world-wide reputation as an expert on municipal transport in large cities and travelled all over the world to advise on questions of organisation and management relating to these enterprises.

On the sale of the West Nile Street property, the Council took active steps to acquire a new home for the Institute. Considerations of finance made it necessary to purchase an existing building and convert it to the needs of the Society. Premises in Bath Street and in Blythswood Square were examined, but from the first the favourite choice was a large house at 218 St Vincent Street, and after a favourable report had been received from Mr John J. Burnet, Architect, the Council recommended to the members the purchase of this property at a price of £9,500; this was agreed to at a special meeting of the Institute held on March 22, 1898. The site was rather farther westward than some members thought convenient, but events have proved that the purchase was fully justified.

Mr John Wilson was at this time President and under his direction plans were prepared by Mr Burnet and the necessary alterations put in hand. The building consisted of three principal floors, attics and a basement, with ground available behind for development. On the ground floor a hall was constructed, occupying the whole depth of the house. The library and the Council room were located on the first floor, and on the floor above examination and class rooms were arranged. With commendable prudence the Council agreed for the time being to let the coach house at the back to the former owner of the building so that he could house there a horse and van used in connection with his business.

No. 218 St Vincent Street was a large and dignified town house and after alteration proved very well suited for its new use. The alterations cost £4,970, and the whole cost of the buildings, alterations and furnishings was upwards of £16,000, which was in those days considered a very substantial sum. The premises were formally opened in the presence of a large and representative gathering at a reception on the afternoon of July 10, 1899. A well-known composite photograph taken in 1900 shows the members of the Institute assembled in their new Hall.

If the Council had seemed to the members dilatory at one time in providing adequate accommodation for the Institute, this charge could not again have been made, because since 1898 they have planned well ahead in the matter of accommodation and successive acquisitions and extensions have been carried through. St Vincent Street is, as is well known, one of the principal business streets in Glasgow and the Institute's premises, towards the top of the hill, are a prominent feature in that locality of the city.

The first extension was in 1915 when two additional class rooms were constructed in the basement and the ventilating and heating of the whole premises were brought up to date. After the First World War, in 1923, when the numbers of members and apprentices were expanding very rapidly, the adjoining property, No. 220, was purchased. The stables and out-buildings at the back of both buildings were removed, and a large and dignified hall, capable of seating about 300, was constructed to the plans of Mr James Miller, A.R.S.A., F.R.I.B.A. At the same time several class rooms, lavatory accommodation and caretakers' houses were constructed, with entrances both from St Vincent Street and from West George Lane. The

THE INSTITUTE'S HALL IN GLASGOW

MEMBERS' ROOM

THE INSTITUTE'S HALL IN GLASGOW

Part of the Library

former hall became the principal room of the library. Mr D. Johnstone Smith was President at this time, and it was largely owing to his great interest and organising ability that these alterations were so successfully completed. The extension was celebrated at a reception to members and two smoking concerts for apprentices.

In 1927 the building No. 224 St Vincent Street was purchased, and during 1932-34 improvements were made in the entrance hall at No. 218 and an access constructed linking Nos. 218 and 220. The ground floor of No. 220 was converted into a reading room for members and the basement became an apprentices' room; at the same time facilities for light refreshments were provided. No. 224 remained let for the time being to various office tenants, and in 1934 No. 226 was also acquired for future development. By this purchase, the Institute became the owner of the whole block of buildings up to Blythswood Street with ample room for extension when the need arose.

After the Second World War, the Tutorial Classes Committee found that further class room and students' accommodation had become an urgent necessity, and in 1948 the Council decided to put in hand another scheme of alteration, this time at No. 224. Plans were prepared by Messrs Frank Burnet & Boston, Architects, and the whole interior of this building was reconstructed into six large class rooms on three floors, together with another caretaker's house. At the same time various minor alterations in other parts of the premises and a considerable enlargement of the heating system were carried through. The six new class rooms which were opened in 1950, with their modern furnishings and lighting, are proving of great value in the tutorial work of the Institute and have also been of much assistance in connection with the examinations, at which very large numbers of candidates have now to be accommodated.

When the time came in 1951 for the Glasgow Institute to hand over their possessions to The Institute of Chartered Accountants of Scotland, they could do so with some satisfaction, knowing that they had created a very valuable property on which from first to last a sum of more than £90,000 had been expended. There is available a spacious hall, suitable for public meetings. The needs of apprentices have been met by the provision of ten class rooms accommodating 50 to 200 students each. Accommodation has been provided for reading rooms and for the housing of the caretaking staff. The Council room and library are in the original part of the building; the library occupies the greater part of three floors and also part of the basement. There is adequate office accommodation and some strong-rooms are available for the use of members. The site at No. 226 is available for further extensions if these should be required.

The students' section of the building is in appearance utilitarian, though bright. It is quiet by day, except for the operations of cleaners, but in the evenings, during the tutorial sessions, it becomes a hive of activity. By contrast, the original or main building has an atmosphere of dignity and quietness, contributed to by the rich wood panelling, the soft carpeting of the entrance hall and stairway, the oil paintings of past Presidents and the handsome furnishings. That these buildings occupy a special place in the affections of the members from Glasgow is by no means surprising.

This record would not be complete without some reference to a series of caretakers in whom the Glasgow Institute has been very fortunate. From early in 1874, the premises were in the charge of Colour Serjeant George Adams, who had served with The Black Watch in many parts of the world. He brought to his duties something of the army discipline, order and cleanliness. Surviving representatives of his days remember with a measure of affection the old soldier who at that time guarded the "sacred precincts" from any intrusion by the mere apprentice. It was not unknown for a presumptuous youth to be incontinently expelled from the building at the end of a broom, the veteran's accustomed implement of toil and a handy symbol of authority.

On his retiral in 1909, Adams was succeeded by George

Livie, who had been a Regimental Serjeant Major in The Queen's Own Cameron Highlanders. Mr Livie, whose erect figure and white moustache remain in the memory, also became very well known to a later generation of members and apprentices; his methods were perhaps more persuasive, but he enforced a strict discipline within the buildings in his day, and he had to deal with numbers far exceeding those in the days of Adams. On the death of Mr Livie in 1938 he was succeeded as principal caretaker by Mr James R. Cruickshank, late of The Gordon Highlanders, who had joined the staff of the Institute in 1926. Mr Cruickshank in his turn maintains the high traditions of his predecessors and is a watchful guardian of the prestige of the Institute within his now extensive domain.

The library of the Edinburgh Society was founded in 1865. As the Society had then no permanent home its progress was gradual, although books were steadily added and a library room was ultimately obtained and organised for the convenience of members. A catalogue was prepared in 1890.

It was not until the library was removed to 27 Queen Street in 1891 that it began to assume large proportions. From that time it increased rapidly and by the time of the Jubilee of the Society in 1904 it already contained almost all the well-known works on book-keeping and accounts, most of the legal books bearing on the profession, including full sets of both Scottish and English decisions, and a large number of actuarial and economic publications. A classified catalogue of the library was issued in 1902.

In the intervening years the growth of the library has continued. All the sections referred to in the preceding paragraph have been kept up to date by the addition of new works, and extensive sections have been created in taxation, cost accounting and other newer branches of professional activities. There is also included a selection of the most important works published abroad, in particular in the United States of America.

Among the more rare books on book-keeping there are to

be found copies of Paciolo (both editions), Tagliente, Gottlieb, Manzoni, Cardanus, Schweicker, Menher, Rocha, Casanova, Pietra, Petri, Passchier-Goessens, Grisogono, Moschetti, Buingha, Malynes, Carpenter, Dafforne, Flori, Collins, Venturi, Venturoli, Colinson, Hatton, de la Porte, Irson, Roose, and others extending from mediæval times until the present day.

The reading rooms are supplied with a wide selection of periodicals relating to the profession and of the various banking, economic, financial and insurance journals; the daily and weekly newspapers and magazines are also provided.

The Annual Report of 1905 records that in view of the dimensions to which the library had grown and to the increasing use made of it a Librarian, Mr Alfred Fairhurst, had been appointed. In 1906 Mr Fairhurst was succeeded by Mr C. T. E. Phillips, who held the appointment until 1920, when he resigned on his appointment as Librarian to Chetham's Library, Manchester. He was followed by Miss Margaret E. Mitchell, who had acted as assistant to the Secretary and Treasurer since 1918. Miss Mitchell continued to act as Assistant Secretary and Librarian until her retiral in 1948.

Miss Mitchell had a high sense of duty and responsibility and performed her work with painstaking efficiency. She was loyal and trustworthy in all her dealings, and during the difficult years of the Second World War the Society had special reason to be grateful to her for her services. She always had the interests of the Society at heart, and, when she retired after twenty-eight years of devoted service, she was presented with a gift of money contributed by members and apprentices as a token of their goodwill and wishes for her future happiness.

Miss Mitchell was succeeded as Assistant Secretary and Librarian by Mrs B. B. Dale Green, M.B.E.(Mil.), who is now an Assistant Secretary of the amalgamated Institute. The present Librarian is Mr A. W. S. Marshall, C.A.

References to the acquisition of books to form the nucleus of a library are to be found among the earliest minutes of the Glasgow Institute, and one of the objects in hiring rooms from the Stock Exchange Association was to provide a home for these books. A list of the books first purchased has survived and for its curiosity may here be reproduced; it runs as follows:—

Bell's Principles of Scotch Law	£1	1	0
Macallan's Erskine	0	16	0
Erskine's Principles of the Law of Scotland	0	13	6
Burton on Bankruptcy	1	0	0
Session Cases, 32 Vols. to 1854	31	0	0
Thomson on Bills	1	1	0
Ross's Commercial Cases, Vols. 1 & 2	3	3	0
Fraser's Personal and Domestic Law, 2 Vols.	1	18	0
Shaw's Digest, 3 Vols.	7	7	0
More's Stair's Institutions of the Law of Scotland, 2 Vols.	2	5	0
Smith's Mercantile Law	1	12	6
Jones on Annuities, 2 Vols.	0	13	6
Price on Annuities	0	10	6
De Morgan on Probabilities	0	3	0
Quetelet on Probabilities	0	1	0
Morgan on Annuities	0	10	6
Thomson on Entails	0	9	0
	£54	4	6

These purchases were approved by the Council in April 1856, but despite this promising start it does not appear that much progress was made for a time, because a corresponding list prepared in 1861 shows only about five or six additions—one of which, however, was a book on the Law of Bankruptcy in England. The books, according to a minute, were "lying in a press in the upper room of the Stock Exchange under charge of the porter . . . with whom arrangements had been made to give them out to the members upon application." That this arrangement was not entirely satisfactory may be gathered from a Council minute of 1863 from which it appears that a member had submitted a memorial to the effect that a library of reference for the use of the members be purchased. The Secretary explained that this memorial had evidently been prepared by the member in ignorance of the fact that the Institute already possessed a library.

The memorial may not have been without effect, however,

since from that time onwards there are more frequent references to books purchased for the library and better arrangements for the convenience of members who wished to consult them. There is no doubt however that, as in Edinburgh, it was not until the Institute obtained premises of its own that a marked improvement took place. Once the library was established in the new hall in West Nile Street in 1873, it quickly grew in size and usefulness. A wider range of professional books was soon acquired and there were also added some more general reference books, including THE DICTIONARY OF NATIONAL BIOGRAPHY. The fact that Bankruptcy was still among the predominant interests is evidenced by the purchase about this time of Seyd's RECORD OF FAILURES AND LIQUIDATIONS.

In 1885 the first Library Committee of the Glasgow Institute was formed, the first Convener being, it is thought, Mr J. Wyllie Guild. Under this Committee great progress was made and about 300 additional books were purchased, necessitating the provision of extra shelving in the hall. These books included, in addition to volumes on professional subjects, works on political economy, constitutional history and general history, and also general literature. Foremost in advocating these improvements to the library, and a generous contributor to it, was Mr Wyllie Guild—a dynamic personality and himself an enthusiastic book collector. His donations included a number of early books on accounting and book-keeping and many others of a more general character.

The first catalogue of importance was printed and circulated in 1889; this was compiled by Mr Franklin T. Barrett of Baillie's Institution Free Library.

In 1899, after the Institute had moved to the new premises at 218 St Vincent Street and after a period during which large numbers of books had been added, a valuation of the library was made by Mr Hugh Hopkins, Bookseller. The figure he arrived at was £977, 13s. To-day the library is insured for a large sum, but any figure can only be an estimate of the worth of a collection which is largely irreplaceable.

In 1901 a supplementary catalogue was prepared, and in

1906 a new and very extensive catalogue was completed by Mr John M. Mitchell. This was followed by supplements on three occasions; and during the past four years, after a complete overhaul and the elimination of obsolete and surplus volumes, an entirely fresh catalogue has been prepared on the loose-leaf system; the binders are housed in a suitable cabinet. This work has been carried out, in conjunction with the staff of the Institute, by the late Mr John Fraser and Mr James M. Tait, both of the Mitchell Library, Glasgow. The catalogue is now being printed. At the present time the library contains 15,303 volumes with a borrowing record of 6,639 volumes per annum.

Since the Institute moved to its present location there have been only four Conveners of the Library Committee. The late Mr Charles Ker had been appointed in 1897; he was one of the original members of the Committee in 1885. Mr Ker was succeeded by the late Mr T. A. Craig, who occupied the position for 20 years, and he in turn was succeeded by the late Mr Dugald Bannatyne, whose term of office was 14 years. The present Convener, Mr J. B. Wardhaugh, has presided over the Committee for 19 years.

In 1899, owing to the increasing use being made of the library, it was found necessary to appoint a whole-time assistant. It was only after very careful consideration and consultation that the Council agreed to the appointment of a young woman. She was to attend for eight hours per day and her salary was to be 10s. per week plus—as the minute runs—" one black dress per annum, if found suitable " (whether the dress or the applicant is not entirely clear). In 1902 Miss Mary A. Craig was appointed as Librarian and she faithfully served the Institute in this capacity for the long period of 51 years, during the greater part of which she was in full charge of the Library. Her knowledge of the contents of her library, acquired during her long years of service, was as amazing as her ability to recognise, perhaps after years abroad, the former timid apprentice now grown grey-haired and large of build. Miss Craig's successor as Librarian, Miss Agnes C. Gillespie, has been in the service of the Institute for many years, and has had the special advantage of having taken part in the exhaustive re-cataloguing of books which, as mentioned above, has just been completed.

It has recently been decided by the Council that while Edinburgh and Aberdeen will retain their libraries and will indeed add to them as the need arises, the principal library of the Institute shall be the Glasgow library. This decision has been made largely on the grounds of economy, and it will be open to all members of the Institute in the United Kingdom to borrow books—by post if need be—from the Glasgow library. Some notes on the scope of the library may not therefore be out of place.

Although the library is primarily a professional one, it is not confined solely to professional literature but embraces, with certain restrictions, non-professional books. The policy of successive committees has been to add every new book of importance relating directly or indirectly to the work of an accountant and new editions of standard works. The needs of apprentice students have always been kept in mind and a liberal number of copies of the standard text books most useful to them is maintained. Subject to these priorities, it has been the practice to acquire general literature mainly in the categories of history, biography, travel, social affairs, etc., but to exclude politics, religion and fiction. It is not an exaggeration to say that of professional literature everything of importance to accountants, including a wide series of law books, is available. In addition to text books, the library contains the official Law Reports from early years—House of Lords, Court of Session, Queen's Bench Division and Court of Appeal, Tax Cases and the Digests relating thereto. Statutory instruments are covered by HALSBURY'S STATUTORY INSTRUMENTS and BUTTERWORTH'S EMERGENCY LEGISLATION; Parliamentary proceedings are covered by HANSARD (weekly and collated issues), and KEESING'S CONTEMPORARY ARCHIVES provide a handy digest of current affairs. Information on investment matters is available in the card index cabinet containing the Exchange Telegraph Company's Daily Statistics. In the reading room current numbers of all the more important professional and other periodicals are provided.

It is difficult in a few words to give an adequate idea of the non-professional section of the library, which contains a wealth of interesting literature and must provide something to suit most tastes. Mention may be made of the following more unusual items: the publications of The Maitland Club, The Bannatyne Club, The Scottish History Society, and The Navy Records Society; Sir William Fraser's Works on Scottish Families; THE DICTIONARY OF NATIONAL BIOGRAPHY (65 volumes) and the CAMBRIDGE HISTORIES (Ancient, Mediæval and British Empire). There is also an extensive collection of books on Old Glasgow and a large series of local and family histories.

The collection of rarer and more valuable books, while not so extensive as that in Edinburgh, contains, among others, RECORD'S ARITHMETIC (1658), COCKER'S ARITHMETIC (1678), FOSTER'S ARITHMETIC (1673), a Dutch Bible of 1642 and an Erasmus of 1544, THE NAVAL CHRONICLE (1799 to 1818), PENNANT'S TOUR OF SCOTLAND (1776) and Acts of the Scots Parliaments (1124 to 1707). There are also some of the earliest works on book-keeping, including GUIDE TO BOOK-KEEPING BY WAY OF DR. AND CR. by Thomas King (1717), BOOK-KEEPING METHODISED by John Mair (1736) and INTRODUCTION TO MERCHANDISE by Professor Robert Hamilton, LL.D. (1799).

From the foregoing pages it will be seen that the members of the Institute, wherever they may be, have good reason to be proud of their premises and libraries and that in these as in other respects the objects of the founders a century ago have been well achieved.

CHAPTER IX

RETROSPECT AND PROSPECT

THE reader who has perused this book thus far will have read of the origins and early history of accountancy in Britain; of the origins and history of the professional bodies which are now The Institute of Chartered Accountants of Scotland; and of the developments during the past hundred years in the functions which accountants perform and the techniques which they employ. The task of the author of this chapter is to contemplate and contrast the developments that have taken place over the past century and to consider the present with an eye to the future.

The fundamentals have not changed, in that the purpose of the accountancy profession is to serve the community in which we live. At the end of the last chapter of THE HISTORY OF ACCOUNTING AND ACCOUNTANTS the author, fifty years ago, wrote: "If we read the signs of the times aright a far greater development all over the world awaits the profession during the next fifty years than that which we have witnessed during the half century which has just elapsed." How right he was. At that time it was estimated that the total number of accountants in the world who were members of recognised Societies was only some 11,000, of whom about one half were in the United Kingdom and only five per cent were in the United States of America. The membership of the recognised bodies of public accountants of Great Britain alone now numbers over 40,000: there is one accountant to every 1,250 of the population in Great Britain and one to every 3,000 of the population in the United States. The rate at which the profession has grown during the past half century is remarkable, but if the experience of Great Britain is any guide, the period of growth of the profession throughout the world is by no means ended.

The hundred years that the Scottish Institute has just completed have been marked by many changes. One of the most important milestones in the history of Scottish chartered accountants was the setting up of the General Examining Board in 1892. A little later, before the beginning of the present century, the movement of Scottish chartered accountants to England and elsewhere had begun, and it says much for the foresight of some of the earlier members who had gone to London that the three separate Scottish bodies of accountants came together in 1898 to form The Association of Scottish Chartered Accountants in London, which might almost be said to have shown an example which the parent bodies did not emulate for over fifty years.

There is no doubt that the passing of the Companies Act in 1900 brought a great influx of work to accountants, and since then accountants have played a wider part in the every-day life and work of the communities they serve. We can see in these last fifty years the beginning and extension of the employment of large numbers of accountants in Government service and the increased movement of members of the profession into industry and commerce. These trends were largely due to the services rendered by accountants to Government Departments during the First and Second World Wars, which made Civil Servants and industrialists realise more fully the extent of the assistance which the trained accountant can bring to their problems. Indeed, it is difficult nowadays to conceive how the machinery of Government and of industry and commerce could continue to function without the services which accountants provide.

There is no doubt that the relationship between the accountant and his client has greatly changed over the last century, especially in the more personal businesses; now the client looks upon his auditor or his accountant as his guide, philosopher and friend to an extent quite unknown fifty years ago. Doubtless this is due to the greater complexity of business these days and not a little due to the problems and impact of taxation. Fifty years ago the apprentice chartered accountant knew little about taxation, and even for the qualified accountant taxation had no problems.

The first real upheaval during the last half century was the First World War. There was no compulsory military service at the start, but many accountants and apprentices and members of the office staffs were in the Territorial Army or volunteered for service, and many gave their lives in the awful carnage of trench warfare. That war necessitated much improvisation to enable the work of the profession to be continued and it was then that the employment of women in accountants' offices greatly increased.

It was during the First World War that it was realised that co-operation among the three Societies of Scottish chartered accountants was necessary and a Joint Committee of Councils was set up which functioned until the amalgamation in 1951. That Joint Committee's powers were very limited, but it is due to their setting up, during the Second World War, a committee to work out a scheme of amalgamation that the happy co-ordination of the profession in Scotland has been brought about. It may seem strange that it took two World Wars to bring a united profession in Scotland into being.

After 1918 the rôle and function of the accountant showed rapid change, due partly to the impact of taxation and partly to the advancement of the knowledge of the services accountants could render, particularly in the realms of costing, business management and finance, and it was following the First World War that women were admitted to membership of the profession. There was a time about 1930 when there seemed almost to be a surplus of accountants and it looked—temporarily at least—as if the profession was overcrowded. Fortunately, many practitioners were sufficiently optimistic to continue to encourage young men to go in for the profession, because they fully believed there were bright prospects ; it was well that this was done, as by the time the Second World War began the number of accountants available was quite inadequate. The impact of the Second World War was immediate, and it can certainly be said that the profession rendered most valuable assistance to the Government in its various Ministries and Departments.

If we view the last fifty or sixty years through the eyes of an accountant who has been in practice during that period we will see the extraordinary changes which have taken place. Sixty years ago the tools of the profession consisted largely of a red and a blue pencil. The rubber stamp hardly existed. Typewriters were almost non-existent. All the copying of balance sheets and accounts was done by male clerks whose copperplate writing would be a valuable example to many a young man to-day. In those days there were practically no typewriters, and where they were installed they were operated by men. There were no women employed in accountants' offices ; such things as internal telephones did not exist, and probably there was only one national telephone installed in a booth somewhere in the offices.

Sir Winston Churchill in one of his addresses said: "The great mass of human beings, absorbed in the toils, cares and activities of life, are only dimly conscious of the pace at which mankind has begun to travel. We look back a hundred years, and see that great changes have taken place. We look back fifty years, and see that the speed is constantly quickening." He went on to say that it is science that has produced this new prodigious speed in man. That can truly be said to have affected the accountancy profession. It has produced a speed of transport that enables us to carry out work in distant places with a facility never previously dreamed of. It has produced accounting machines and calculators of all kinds and descriptions, and it would require someone given the imagination such as was given to Lord Tennyson in *Locksley Hall*, where he wrote :

> *When I dipt into the future, far as human eye could see ;*
> *Saw the Vision of the world, and all the wonder that would be—*

to foretell what further advances will be made. It seems that we are moving to the age of more machinery, electric and otherwise, and within the reasonably foreseeable future it is possible that book-keeping and books as we now know them will hardly exist. Even now records are made on punched cards, microfilm or electric recording tape. The effect on auditing of some of these developments has not yet been fully worked out, and what the future will hold it is difficult to foretell. Certainly full utilisation of some of the developments in the field of electronics which are now within the bounds of practical possibility may mean changes in our company law on such matters as requirements with regard to the books to be kept.

What is the future of auditing is uncertain. Much of the work of the auditor concerns the past. Much valuable time and labour is thus expended—doubtless for the protection of the shareholder—but in many cases can it truly be said that the audit does really help the efficiency and the output of industry? What industry wants is forecasts and guidance for its future policy.

It may be that, in the larger businesses at any rate, the auditor will have to rely more on the internal auditor and the efficiency of the internal check system, and devote himself more and more to the "efficiency" audit. A new problem will arise for the profession in laying down methods and standards for the "efficiency" audit.

Recent years have shown many significant changes in the profession. Vast numbers of accountants have abandoned the field of private practice and have gone to work in industry, where the inducements and prospects seem greater. We have also seen the Nationalised industries absorbing large numbers of accountants. One factor which has had great bearing on these movements is doubtless the prospect of pensionable employment. With the present high rates of taxation and in the present state of taxation law it is virtually impossible to-day for a young professional man who is self-employed to save out of income enough money to provide for eventual retirement. If things remain as they are the great majority of the self-employed must expect to die in harness unless they have inherited capital or have been able to save money before the rise in income tax at the beginning of the Second World War. These facts are a source of concern not only to accountants but to all those other professions in which private practice is both a necessity for the carrying on of the profession's work in the way in which we understand it to-day and also an indispensable training ground for each new generation of students as they come forward with a view to qualifying. So far no Chancellor of the Exchequer has had the courage, or possibly the financial resources, to enable the self-employed man to make adequate provision for his old age, but in February 1954 the Departmental Committee on Retirement Benefits, after some years of most careful study, produced a Report which contains detailed recommendations on the whole subject. One can only hope that effect will be given to these proposals before very long.

It can be said that accountants to-day have a place in the community which is not without honour and that, at least as far as the United Kingdom is concerned, they are looked upon as giving valuable, and indeed essential, help in carrying on the financial administration of the country. It therefore devolves on us who have inherited many advantages from our predecessors to consider our responsibilities and the claims which the future has upon us, particularly in regard to our methods of training for the profession. Here there is a great danger and, occupied as we are with other cares and responsibilities, we must be sure that our eyes are open to it. Our lot is cast in the age of the specialist and there is a natural temptation to allow young people to specialise too early and too closely. One feels that a great responsibility now falls on all who are interested in the education and training for the profession: we must have a clear appreciation that it is essential to insist upon a broad general education and also a broad training, and we must guard against any concentrated or narrow specialisation until after a sound general grounding has been acquired. Our danger would lie in the intensifying of subject study and in the abandoning of the broad and general training for the profession. Broad practical experience is the essential; specialisation must come after. We believe that the apprenticeship system, whereby the apprentice must serve his apprenticeship in the offices of practising members, is the best method of providing the fundamental training of the accountant, and we must guard against any attempt to abandon that basic system in favour of any other method of training, however superficially attractive that other method may be.

In the United Kingdom the accountancy profession differs from law, medicine and certain other professions in that the accountancy profession is not "closed": anyone without any qualifications whatsoever can in the United Kingdom "put up his plate" and call himself an accountant, although he cannot, of course, call himself "chartered accountant," "incorporated accountant" or "certified accountant" unless he is a member of one or other of the leading accountancy bodies. It is perhaps curious that it is a criminal offence for an unqualified man to pretend to be a doctor or a solicitor but that there is nothing wrong in his pretending to be an accountant. In fact, however, the situation is not as bad as it would appear at first sight, since those who are concerned with government, commerce and industry are for the most part well aware that in the field of public accountancy the accountancy bodies which are recognised by the Board of Trade under section 161 of the Companies Act, 1948, for the purpose of appointment as auditors of public companies are The Institute of Chartered Accountants of Scotland, The Institute of Chartered Accountants in England and Wales, The Institute of Chartered Accountants in Ireland, The Society of Incorporated Accountants and Auditors and The Association of Certified and Corporate Accountants. Membership of these bodies also carries with it practical, if not legal, recognition in many other fields, in some of which those bodies are joined by The Institute of Municipal Treasurers and Accountants and The Institute of Cost and Works Accountants. Due recognition is also given by the Board of Trade, and in other quarters, to qualifications on similar standards obtained overseas by accountants who come to the United Kingdom, and it can be said that the

THE INSTITUTE'S HALL IN GLASGOW

THE MAIN HALL

ONE OF THE INSTITUTE'S TUTORIAL CLASSES IN SESSION—GLASGOW

accountancy profession in the United Kingdom is open to all duly qualified accountants from whatever part of the world they come and without distinction of race, creed or colour.

Nevertheless the five "recognised" bodies of public accountants have doubted for many years whether the present position is wholly satisfactory so far as concerns accountants trained in the United Kingdom, as there is nothing to prevent anyone from forming a new body of accountants with a high-sounding name but with little or no certainty that its members will possess any recognisable professional standards of competence. The problem has been carefully studied for a long period and various proposals have been considered for "closing" the profession so that only those who have been properly trained and tested by examination would be able to practise as public accountants. The difficulties have, however, proved insuperable: the accountancy profession has grown so fast and its ramifications and specialisations have spread so widely that it is impracticable to define with the particularity that would be required for legal purposes any precise boundaries between the proper fields of the accountant and those of other professions such as lawyers, engineers, bankers and others. At the present stage in the profession's history it seems that the most that could be achieved immediately would be to amend section 161 of the Companies Act, 1948, so as to require every company incorporated under that Act to appoint as its auditor a duly qualified practising accountant, and to make statutory the list of the bodies to which such accountants must belong before they can be considered eligible for appointment as auditors, due provision of course being made to protect the rights of accountants who may come from overseas to practise in the United Kingdom. Representations in this sense have indeed been made to the Board of Trade and it is understood that the possibility of introducing legislation on these lines is being studied.

Meanwhile the five "recognised" bodies continue to work together in close and happy co-operation for the benefit of the accountancy profession as a whole.

The accountancy profession has a proud and honourable record. A great profession has been built up by the foresight, labour and sacrifice of its members and without subsidy or doles from any Government or other body for the education of its members.

From this time forth the Scottish Institute has no more to do with her first century. It is her second century she enters upon with a proud record of the past and with great encouragement for the future. We pass on to our successors a live and flourishing Institute, adequately housed and well equipped, and free to carry on the traditions of the past.

APPENDICES

CONTENTS

APPENDIX I

COUNCIL 1954-55

JOHN LIVINGSTON SOMERVILLE, F.R.S.E., *President*
Sir IAN FREDERICK CHENEY BOLTON, Bt., O.B.E., L.L., J.P., *Vice-President*
THOMSON SMITH AIKMAN, B.Com.
NORMAN JOHN BIRD, F.C.W.A.
Professor ROBERT BROWNING, M.A., LL.B.
JAMES CAMPBELL DAVIES, M.C., T.D.
WILLIAM INNES FRENCH, D.S.O., O.B.E., T.D.
JOHN GRAHAM GIRDWOOD, C.B.E.
SEPTIMUS ERIK HOUSTOUN, M.A.
PETER McGREGOR JACKSON
JOHN HERBERT JOHNSTON
ROBERT GARDNER JOHNSON KIRK
NORVAL MURRAY LINDSAY
THOMAS LISTER, M.A.
CHARLES ROWCLIFFE MUNRO
CHARLES GEORGE MICHAEL PEARSON
STANLEY GORDON YORK POOL
CHARLES REID, D.S.O., M.A.
EDWARD BIRNIE REID, O.B.E., T.D.
FREDERICK ALEXANDER RITSON, J.P., F.S.A.
ANDREW RITCHIE TEMPLETON
GRAHAM AITCHISON USHER, M.B.E., T.D.
JAMES ALEXANDER WALKER, C.B.E.

APPENDIX II

CENTENARY COMMITTEE

THE PRESIDENT AND VICE-PRESIDENT

Professor ROBERT BROWNING, M.A., LL.B.
W. I. FRENCH, D.S.O., O.B.E., T.D. (*Convener*)
J. G. GIRDWOOD, C.B.E.
P. M. JACKSON
CHARLES R. MUNRO
JAMES A. WALKER, C.B.E.

LADIES COMMITTEE

Mrs THOMSON S. AIKMAN
Mrs ROBERT BROWNING
Mrs J. CAMPBELL DAVIES
Mrs C. D. GAIRDNER
Mrs J. G. GIRDWOOD
LADY ALLAN HAY
Mrs P. M. JACKSON
Mrs J. H. JOHNSTON
Mrs R. G. J. KIRK
Mrs NORVAL M. LINDSAY
Mrs THOMAS LISTER
Mrs E. H. V. McDOUGALL
Mrs ANDREW W. MUDIE
Mrs CHARLES R. MUNRO
Mrs C. G. M. PEARSON
Mrs S. GORDON Y. POOL
Mrs E. BIRNIE REID
Mrs JOHN L. SOMERVILLE (*Convener*)
Mrs ANDREW R. TEMPLETON
Mrs JAMES A. WALKER
Mrs J. J. WELCH

CENTENARY BALL—JOINT SUB-COMMITTEE

Representatives of The Chartered Accountants Students' Society of Edinburgh :—

W. S. CHARLES (*Convener*)
J. S. FORBES MACDONALD
HUGH MCMICHAEL (*Hon. Secretary*)
H. FORBES MURPHY

Representatives of The Glasgow Chartered Accountants Students' Society :—

R. HUNTER FORBES
HERBERT W. RUSSELL

Representing the Institute's Centenary Committee :—

E. H. V. McDOUGALL

CENTENARY GOLF COMPETITION SUB-COMMITTEE

R. G. J. KIRK
R. IAN MARSHALL
W. A. WHITELAW (*Convener*)

CENTENARY EXHIBITION SUB-COMMITTEE

C. G. M. PEARSON
J. B. WARDHAUGH

Honorary Public Relations Officer :—
DEREK DU PRÉ

Centenary Administrative Assistant :—
Mrs ROSEMARY V. HALL

APPENDIX III

THE INSTITUTE'S STAFF

SECRETARY OF THE INSTITUTE

EARDLEY HAROLD VICTOR McDOUGALL

ASSISTANT SECRETARIES

Mrs BARBARA BOWES DALE GREEN, M.B.E.(Mil.)
THOMAS ROBERTSON MOFFAT, C.A.

LOCAL SECRETARIES

Edinburgh—E. H. V. McDOUGALL, 27 Queen Street, 2 (*Tel.* CENtral 3687)
Glasgow—WILLIAM L. DAVIDSON, C.A., 142 St Vincent Street, C.2 (*Tel.* CITy 6976)
Aberdeen—L. M. DAVIDSON, T.D., C.A., 6 Golden Square (*Tel.* 29073)
Dundee—DONALD B. GRANT, C.A., 22 Meadowside (*Tel.* 6163)
Inverness—W. J. MEIKLEJOHN, C.A., 19 Church Street (*Tel.* 1938)
London—J. WOOD, C.A., 34 Clement's Lane, Lombard Street, E.C.4 (*Tel.* MINcing Lane 1534)

LIBRARIANS

Miss AGNES C. GILLESPIE (Glasgow)
A. W. S. MARSHALL, C.A. (Edinburgh)
GORDON J. INNES, C.A. (Aberdeen)

OTHER MEMBERS OF THE STAFF

Edinburgh

Miss J. M. BICKERTON
Miss S. CAMPBELL PENNEY, M.A.
Miss A. L. COWAN
Miss G. M. DICK
Miss N. M. ELLIS
Miss F. H. FERENBACH
Miss C. A. HAMILTON
Miss K. B. HANNA, M.A.
Miss M. HARKES
Miss N. F. KING
Miss P. A. McINTYRE
Miss M. G. SUTHERLAND
T. TAYLOR
Miss C. M. WILKINSON

Glasgow

Miss MARY B. KNOPP
Miss JANET TENNENT
J. CRUIKSHANK
D. R. McRAE
A. PATE
Mrs R. GARLAND
Mrs S. GROGAN

APPENDIX IV

PAST OFFICE-BEARERS

The Society of Accountants in Edinburgh

Presidents

1853-1864 James Brown
1864-1868 Thomas Mansfield
1869-1876 Chas. Murray Barstow
1876-1879 Charles Pearson
1879-1882 Ralph Erskine Scott
1882-1888 Geo. Auldjo Jamieson
1888-1889 Jas. M. Macandrew, F.F.A.
1889-1892 Thos. Goldie Dickson, F.F.A.
1892-1895 James Howden, F.F.A.
1895-1898 James Haldane
1898-1901 David Pearson, F.F.A.
1901-1904 Hugh Blair
1904-1907 Fred. Walter Carter
1907-1909 J.A.Robertson-Durham, F.F.A.
1910-1913 Robert Cockburn Millar
1913-1916 William Home Cook
1916-1918 Richard Brown
1918-1922 Jas. McKerrell Brown
1922-1925 John M. Howden, D.L., J.P.
1925-1928 C. E. W. Macpherson
1928-1931 Wm. Greenhill
1931-1934 C. J. Shiells
1934-1937 H. W. Haldane
1937-1939 Sir Thomas B. Whitson, D.L., LL.D., F.R.S.E., J.P.
1939-1942 Prof. Wm. Annan, M.A., F.C.W.A.
1942-1945 John M. Geoghegan
1945-1948 J. A. Falconer
1948-1951 R. G. Simpson, M.C.

Secretaries

1853-1863 Alex. Weir Robertson
1863-1892 James Howden, F.F.A.
1892-1916 Richard Brown
1916-1919 T. P. Laird, M.A.
1919-1939 L. B. Bell
1939-1947 Alex. Harrison
1947-1951 James A. Walker, C.B.E.

Treasurers

1853-1863 Kenneth Mackenzie
1863-1879 Alex. Weir Robertson
1879-1892 William Wood
1892-1916 Richard Brown
1916-1919 T. P. Laird, M.A.
1919-1939 L. B. Bell
1939-1947 Alex. Harrison
1947-1951 James A. Walker, C.B.E.

APPENDICES

The Institute of Accountants and Actuaries in Glasgow

Presidents

1853-1864 James McClelland
1864-1867 Peter White
1867-1870 Walter Mackenzie
1870-1876 William Anderson
1876-1878 George Robson
1878-1881 J. Wyllie Guild
1881-1884 John Graham
1884-1887 Alexander Moore
1887-1890 John E. Watson
1890-1894 Walter Mackenzie
1894-1897 James Hutton
1897-1900 John Wilson
1900-1903 Andrew S. McClelland
1903-1906 Thomas Jackson
1906-1909 John Mann, Sen.
1909-1912 Alexander Sloan
1912-1915 Robert Carswell
1915-1918 Alexander Moore
1918-1920 David Strathie
1920-1922 Sir Robert C. Mackenzie, K.B.E., C.B., D.L.
1922-1924 D. Johnstone Smith, LL.D.
1924-1926 Charles Ker, M.A., LL.D.
1926-1928 Sir John M. Macleod, Bt., D.L., LL.D.
1928-1930 Peter Rintoul
1930-1932 David A. Richmond
1932-1934 Sir Thomas Kelly, D.L., LL.D., J.P.
1934-1936 William H. Goff
1936-1938 Matthew Mitchell
1938-1940 Sir Andrew Macharg
1940-1942 D. Norman Sloan, B.L.
1942-1944 James M. Davies
1944-1946 Sir David Allan Hay, K.B.E.
1946-1948 John Duncan
1948-1950 Sir Ian F. C. Bolton, Bt., O.B.E., L.L., J.P.
1950-1951 John F. Carson, O.B.E. (Mil.), V.D.

Secretaries

1853-1867 Walter Mackenzie
1867-1873 J. Wyllie Guild
1873-1909 Alexander Sloan
1909-1940 D. Norman Sloan, B.L.
1940-1951 William L. Davidson

Treasurers

1853-1864 Peter White
1864-1880 Robert McCowan
1881-1894 J. Wyllie Guild
1894-1898 Walter Mackenzie
1898-1900 W. A. Guild
1900-1918 T. A. Craig
1918-1924 Alexander Moore
1924-1934 D. Johnstone Smith, LL.D.
1934-1940 David A. Richmond
1940-1944 Sir Andrew Macharg
1944-1946 John D. Ross
1946-1951 Andrew Craig

APPENDICES

The Society of Accountants in Aberdeen

Presidents

1867-1869 John Smith
1869-1871 George Marquis
1871-1873 Alexander Brand
1873-1875 James A. Sinclair (later 16th Earl of Caithness)
1875-1877 Robert Fletcher
1877-1879 William Lunan
1879-1881 John Crombie
1881-1883 William Milne
1883-1885 James Tytler
1885-1887 Harvey Hall
1887-1889 James Milne, Sen.
1889-1890 Alexander Machray
1890-1896 Alexander Ledingham
1896-1903 George G. Whyte
1903-1907 James Milne
1907-1911 George McBain
1911-1920 Walter A. Reid, LL.D., F.F.A.
1920-1923 John McBain
1923-1926 James A. Jeffrey
1926-1929 Charles Williamson, M.A.
1929-1932 A. S. Mitchell
1932-1935 Herbert H. Bower
1935-1937 John R. Flockhart
1937-1946 John Reid, M.A.
1946-1948 John M. Dunn
1948-1950 William F. Newlands
1950-1951 Gordon J. Innes

Secretaries and Treasurers

1867-1892 James Meston
1892-1911 Walter A. Reid, LL.D., F.F.A.
1911-1937 John Reid, M.A.
1937-1951 L. M. Davidson, T.D.

The Institute of Chartered Accountants of Scotland

Presidents

1951-1952 R. G. Simpson, M.C.
1952-1953 Sir David Allan Hay, K.B.E.

APPENDIX V

PROFESSORS OF ACCOUNTANCY—PAST AND PRESENT

In the University of Edinburgh

THOMAS PATRICK LAIRD, M.A., C.A., 1919-27
WILLIAM ANNAN, M.A., C.A., F.C.W.A., 1927-43
ADAM GEORGE MURRAY, M.A., C.A., 1945-

In the University of Glasgow

JOHN LOUDON, M.A., C.A., 1926-38
IAN WILSON MACDONALD, M.A., C.A., 1938-50
ROBERT BROWNING, M.A., LL.B., C.A., 1950-

APPENDIX VI

DIRECTORS OF STUDIES—PAST AND PRESENT

Glasgow:	1923-1943	THOMAS HART, C.A.
	1944-1950	ROBERT BROWNING, M.A., LL.B., C.A.
	1950-	A. D. PATON, C.A.
Edinburgh:	1924-1934	JOHN E. DALGLIESH, C.A.
	1934-1937	Vacant
	1938-	W. C. TAYLOR, C.A.
London:	1924-1954	J. WOOD, C.A.
	1954-	W. R. S. RITCHIE, C.A.
Aberdeen:	1952-1953	J. W. IRVINE-FORTESCUE, M.A., C.A.
	1953-	W. STUART, M.A. C.A.
Dundee:	1953-	DONALD B. GRANT, C.A.

APPENDIX VII

STATISTICS OF APPRENTICESHIP AND MEMBERSHIP

Royal Charters were originally granted to The Society of Accountants in Edinburgh in 1854, to The Institute of Accountants and Actuaries in Glasgow in 1855, and to The Society of Accountants in Aberdeen in 1867. At the time of the application for their respective Royal Charters, the numbers in the Edinburgh Society were 61, in the Glasgow Institute 49, and in the Aberdeen Society 12—a total of 122 practising Accountants.

The following statistics are designed to show the growth in the number of members and apprentices.

Year	No. of Indentures Registered				No. of Members Admitted				No. of Members at December 31			
	Edinburgh	Glasgow	Aberdeen	Total	Edinburgh	Glasgow	Aberdeen	Total	Edinburgh	Glasgow	Aberdeen	Total
1864	8	*	..	..	6	0	..	6	89	57	..	146
1874	12	*	1	..	3	0	2	5	113	67	15	195
1884	21	*	2	..	14	4	1	19	179	118	20	317
1894	23	*	6	..	11	21	1	33	289	223	30	542
1900	28	57	6	91	13	21	2	36	351	330	39	720
1901	32	67	7	106	17	23	5	45	364	349	44	757
1902	37	56	5	98	16	22	3	41	372	373	45	790
1903	36	69	4	109	19	38	4	61	388	406	48	842
1904	30	73	6	109	29	41	0	70	411	442	46	906
1905	44	79	4	127	27	39	1	67	429	479	47	955
1906	42	79	3	124	17	23	6	46	433	499	52	984
1907	35	90	13	148	18	43	2	63	449	540	52	1041
1908	38	67	5	110	20	41	3	64	466	575	54	1095
1909	44	93	5	142	19	45	4	68	479	615	57	1151
1910	45	109	5	159	24	55	4	83	497	666	61	1224
1911	33	96	3	132	32	49	7	88	523	707	68	1298
1912	27	73	5	105	25	55	2	82	541	752	68	1361

* Unknown

Year	No. of Indentures Registered				No. of Members Admitted				No. of Members at December 31			
	Edinburgh	Glasgow	Aberdeen	Total	Edinburgh	Glasgow	Aberdeen	Total	Edinburgh	Glasgow	Aberdeen	Total
1913	29	93	8	130	29	49	3	81	566	795	71	1432
1914	36	102	5	143	26	38	4	68	580	826	75	1481
1915	21	76	4	101	16	23	3	42	588	830	75	1493
1916	24	52	3	79	10	14	1	25	584	824	74	1482
1917	11	46	2	59	3	10	1	14	574	818	73	1465
1918	15	61	2	78	8	20	1	29	564	823	74	1461
1919	100	185	11	296	22	50	1	73	577	867	75	1519
1920	86	197	16	299	58	122	7	187	630	975	81	1686
1921	81	191	13	285	20	93	4	117	643	1062	83	1788
1922	89	232	11	332	33	79	9	121	668	1132	92	1892
1923	91	218	14	323	38	84	7	129	702	1206	98	2006
1924	94	266	18	378	43	105	8	156	737	1301	106	2144
1925	50	154	7	211	50	119	10	179	783	1403	115	2301
1926	61	170	24	255	42	92	7	141	814	1478	119	2411
1927	63	154	10	227	44	114	6	164	848	1576	125	2549
1928	65	148	12	225	58	140	10	208	899	1704	135	2738
1929	68	176	16	260	69	131	16	216	952	1825	150	2927
1930	63	198	15	276	62	154	19	235	1005	1964	169	3138
1931	77	194	16	287	48	162	6	216	1040	2108	174	3322
1932	76	207	12	295	59	141	11	211	1085	2223	184	3492
1933	60	172	10	242	48	106	6	160	1118	2316	189	3623
1934	46	169	15	230	43	124	10	177	1148	2394	192	3734
1935	39	153	10	202	64	137	9	210	1206	2511	199	3916
1936	48	117	7	172	51	121	9	181	1237	2601	207	4045
1937	32	106	7	145	56	137	9	202	1277	2717	212	4206
1938	50	123	7	180	47	142	5	194	1309	2832	217	4358
1939	42	138	10	190	38	112	11	161	1334	2919	224	4477
1940	41	128	8	177	30	98	9	137	1342	2986	228	4556
1941	34	115	6	155	12	39	2	53	1338	2998	229	4565
1942	26	88	3	117	5	30	2	37	1330	3000	228	4558

Year	No. of Indentures Registered				No. of Members Admitted				No. of Members at December 31			
	Edinburgh	Glasgow	Aberdeen	Total	Edinburgh	Glasgow	Aberdeen	Total	Edinburgh	Glasgow	Aberdeen	Total
1943	20	80	3	103	4	19	0	23	1302	2985	226	4513
1944	21	97	11	129	3	21	0	24	1280	2976	222	4478
1945	31	116	4	151	7	39	2	48	1262	2982	222	4466
1946	57	222	9	288	31	118	7	156	1267	3067	224	4558
1947	86	314	12	412	47	105	13	165	1283	3122	234	4639
1948	107	292	19	418	57	159	11	227	1325	3255	243	4823
1949	74	247	14	335	38	130	6	174	1350	3326	248	4924
1950	101	241	17	359	45	146	5	196	1373	3447	251	5071
1951				283				191				5181
1952				281				239				5349
1953				305				243				5515

APPENDIX VIII

EXAMINATION STATISTICS

	Entrants	Passed
1894		
Intermediate	86	62
Final	29	18
	115	80
1913		
Intermediate	204	92
Final—Whole Division	123	40
1st Division	58	14
2nd Division	81	35
	466	181
1920		
Intermediate	378	250
Final—Whole Division	142	75
1st Division	66	46
2nd Division	95	65
	681	436
1938		
Intermediate—1st Division	330	180
2nd Division	212	136
Final—1st Division	289	171
2nd Division	361	145
	1,192	632
1946		
Intermediate—1st Division	245	126
2nd Division	253	161
Final—1st Division	307	259
2nd Division	255	97
	1,060	643

	Entrants	Passed
1947		
Intermediate—1st Division	375	185
2nd Division	435	247
Final—1st Division	360	279
2nd Division	487	244
	1,657	955
1948		
Intermediate—1st Division	526	228
2nd Division	706	328
Final—1st Division	362	225
2nd Division	548	187
	2,142	1,022
1949		
Intermediate—1st Division	503	265
2nd Division	693	379
Final—1st Division	513	321
2nd Division	610	179
	2,319	1,144
1950		
Intermediate—1st Division	539	291
2nd Division	555	275
Final—1st Division	561	287
2nd Division	631	210
	2,286	1,063
1951		
Intermediate—1st Division	485	273
2nd Division	557	282
Final—1st Division	509	250
2nd Division	698	282
	2,249	1,087

	Entrants	Passed
1952		
Intermediate—1st Division	459	232
2nd Division	507	307
Final—1st Division	560	295
2nd Division	739	213
	2,265	1,047
1953		
Intermediate—1st Division	509	274
2nd Division	432	260
Final—1st Division	515	293
2nd Division	734	261
	2,190	1,088

APPENDIX IX

CENTENARY CELEBRATIONS

To mark the Centenary of The Institute of Chartered Accountants of Scotland the Council of the Institute has arranged a programme of ceremonies and functions in Edinburgh from June 16 to 18, 1954, of which an outline is given below. The leading accountancy bodies throughout the world have been invited to send representatives who will be the Institute's guests on this occasion. At the time or compiling this Appendix the following have accepted such invitations :—

From the British Isles

The Institute of Chartered Accountants in England and Wales
The Institute of Chartered Accountants in Ireland
The Society of Incorporated Accountants and Auditors
The Association of Certified and Corporate Accountants
The Institute of Municipal Treasurers and Accountants
The Institute of Cost and Works Accountants

From Elsewhere

Australia

Australian Society of Accountants
The Institute of Chartered Accountants in Australia

Austria

Kammer der Wirtschaftstreuhänder

Belgium

Collège National des Experts-Comptables de Belgique
Institut Belge des Reviseurs de Banques
Société Royale Chambre Belge des Comptables à Bruxelles

Canada

The Canadian Institute of Chartered Accountants
The Institute of Chartered Accountants of British Columbia
The Institute of Chartered Accountants of Manitoba
The Institute of Chartered Accountants of Ontario
The Institute of Chartered Accountants of Saskatchewan

APPENDICES

Denmark

Foreningen af Statsautoriserede Revisorer

East Africa

The Association of Accountants in East Africa

Finland

K.H.T.-Yhdistys—Föreningen C.G.R.

France

Compagnie Nationale des Experts Comptables
Union Professionnelle de Sociétés Fiduciaires d'Expertise Comptable

Germany

Bundesverband der Vereidigten Buchprüfer
Institut der Wirtschaftsprüfer

India

The Institute of Chartered Accountants of India

Israel

The Association of Public Accountants and Auditors in Israel

Malta

The Malta Institute of Accountants

Netherlands

Nederlands Instituut van Accountants
Vereniging van Academisch Gevormde Accountants

New Zealand

Incorporated Institute of Accountants of New Zealand
The New Zealand Institute of Cost-Accountants
New Zealand Society of Accountants

Norway

Norges Statsautoriserte Revisorers Forening

Philippines

Philippine Institute of Accountants

South Africa

The Cape Society of Accountants and Auditors
Natal Society of Accountants

Southern Rhodesia

Rhodesia Society of Accountants

Sweden

Föreningen Auktoriserade Revisorer
Svenska Revisorsamfundet

Switzerland

Schweizerische Kammer für Revisionswesen

United States of America

American Accounting Association
The American Institute of Accountants
The Institute of Internal Auditors
The California Society of Certified Public Accountants
The Georgia Society of Certified Public Accountants
Illinois Society of Certified Public Accountants
Maine Society of Public Accountants
The Michigan Association of Certified Public Accountants
Nebraska Society of Certified Public Accountants
The New York State Society of Certified Public Accountants
The Ohio Society of Certified Public Accountants
Pennsylvania Institute of Certified Public Accountants
Texas Society of Certified Public Accountants

Uruguay

Colegio de Doctores en Ciencias Económicas y Contadores del Uruguay

APPENDICES

The following is an outline of the programme of the celebrations in Edinburgh :—

Wednesday, June 16, 1954—

Forenoon	SERVICE OF COMMEMORATION AND THANKSGIVING in St Giles' Cathedral (The High Kirk of Edinburgh) to be conducted by The Very Reverend Charles L. Warr, K.C.V.O., D.D., LL.D., Dean of the Thistle and Chapel Royal, with The Right Reverend Bishop K. C. H. Warner, D.S.O., D.D.
Afternoon	LUNCHEON to be given in the Adam Rooms, George Hotel, by the President and Mrs Somerville to entertain some of the Institute's guests from other accountancy bodies.
	OPENING PLENARY SESSION in the Usher Hall to welcome all attending the festivities and to hear congratulatory addresses from representatives of eleven accountancy bodies at home and overseas.
Evening	CENTENARY BANQUET in the Music Hall at the Assembly Rooms.
	LADIES' DINNER in the Adam Rooms, George Hotel.

Thursday, June 17, 1954—

Forenoon and Afternoon	GOLF COMPETITION at Muirfield and Luffness.
	CONDUCTED MOTOR COACH TOUR to the Border Country, including Abbotsford House and Melrose and Dryburgh Abbeys.
Forenoon	CONDUCTED MOTOR COACH TOUR of Edinburgh.
Afternoon	CONDUCTED MOTOR COACH TOUR of Edinburgh, incorporating also a visit to the Forth Bridge.
Evening	CIVIC RECEPTION in the City Chambers by the Lord Provost, Magistrates and Council of the City and Royal Burgh of Edinburgh.
	THEATRE PARTY to the King's Theatre.

Friday, June 18, 1954—

Forenoon — CLOSING PLENARY SESSION in the Music Hall at the Assembly Rooms, at which the following Papers will be delivered :—

"The History and Development of the Accountancy Profession in Scotland," by Professor Robert Browning, M.A., LL.B., C.A., and "The Accountant in Modern Society," by Mr Ian T. Morrow, C.A., F.C.W.A., A.T.I.I.

Afternoon — LUNCHEON to be given in the Adam Rooms, George Hotel, by the President and Mrs Somerville to entertain the rest of the Institute's guests from other accountancy bodies.

LUNCHEON in the Albyn Rooms for Lady Members of the Institute.

CONDUCTED MOTOR COACH TOUR of Edinburgh and district.

MANNEQUIN PARADE in the Adam Rooms, George Hotel.

GOLF FACILITIES for those who wish to play.

Evening — CENTENARY BALL in the Assembly Rooms, organised on behalf of the Institute by The Chartered Accountants Students' Society of Edinburgh and The Glasgow Chartered Accountants Students' Society.

EXHIBITION

From June 14 to June 25 an exhibition dealing with the progress of accounting through the ages will be held in the Institute's premises at 27 Queen Street, Edinburgh, during the hours of 9 A.M. to 7 P.M.

To complete the Centenary Celebrations there are to be held in Glasgow on March 15, 1955, a RECEPTION at the Institute's Hall and a BANQUET at the Central Hotel. The date marks the hundredth anniversary of the grant of the Royal Charter to the former Institute of Accountants and Actuaries in Glasgow.

Printed by William Blackwood & Sons Ltd., Edinburgh

For Product Safety Concerns and Information please contact our EU
representative GPSR@taylorandfrancis.com
Taylor & Francis Verlag GmbH, Kaufingerstraße 24, 80331 München, Germany

www.ingramcontent.com/pod-product-compliance
Ingram Content Group UK Ltd.
Pitfield, Milton Keynes, MK11 3LW, UK
UKHW020157260926
475702UK00047B/552
9780367511883